GARY SINGH

THE SAN JOSE EARTHQUAKES

A SEISMIC SOCCER LEGACY

THE
History
PRESS

Published by The History Press
Charleston, SC 29403
www.historypress.net

Copyright © 2015 by Gary Singh
All rights reserved

First published 2015

Manufactured in the United States

ISBN 978.1.62619.900.2

Library of Congress Control Number: 2014958123

For Alice Singh, who raised me in the stands at Spartan Stadium, and Gary Singh Sr., who never got a chance to rebound.

CONTENTS

ACKNOWLEDGEMENTS

When someone grows up right alongside a sport in his hometown, a lifetime (lifeline?) of thank-you notes begins to emerge. This crudely simplified breakdown into component parts of a much larger system of influence might seem over-elementary to some, because it is. With that disclaimer in mind, this book would not have happened without my interconnectedness to several key individuals.

I am very indebted to Jed Mettee and Frank Stranzl of the San Jose Earthquakes communications team, who graciously let me wander in and out of restricted areas for fourteen years and helped me with all sorts of domestic-American-sports-style statistical knowledge. I am a better writer thanks to their professionalism.

Likewise, I am grateful to Dan Pulcrano, CEO of Metro Newspapers, for allowing me plenty of space to elevate the profile of soccer in San Jose for fourteen straight years when I had no idea I was even accomplishing that, plus all the editors I've ever worked with at that newspaper: Corinne Asturias, Mike Connor, Michael S. Gant, Stett Holbrook, Traci Hukill, Todd Inoue, Eric Johnson, Steve Palopoli, Traci Vogel and Heather Zimmerman. All of them somehow managed to put up with me.

I owe a lot to my editor at The History Press, Will McKay, who was phenomenal to work with from the very beginning. His vision helped bring this project to a smashing conclusion.

Hats go off to Alida Bray, Jim Reed, Ken Middlebrook and Katrina Anderson at History San Jose for all their help, especially their mammoth catalogue of San Jose soccer-related materials. Someday, the U.S. Soccer Hall of Fame will live again, in San Jose—somehow!

On a street level, there exist quite a few characters around San Jose who unconditionally and unintentionally helped this book write itself. Thanks to Teri Nguyen for being the quadrilingual grand cosmic life-virtuoso of the San Jose universe; Danielle, Tori and Tamara at Satori Tea Company, whose Ginger Citrus Guayusa fueled the gonzo-in-retrospect madness required for this narrative; Gretchen Baisa and Julie Kodama at NextSpace Coworking, who supported me with even more tea and Wi-Fi; Apple Man Extraordinaire Dave Burnham for building the Hackintosh on which much of this book was written; Brando Erazo for driving me to Gabbo's grave in order to sign the book contract; Napoleon Badillo, who graciously supplied photos, pro bono, for several of my newspaper columns over the years; Roy's Station, the best coffee shop ever in San Jose; and all the other tea-soaked establishments that allowed me to move in over the years: Caffe Frascati, Philz Coffee, the Fairmont Lobby Lounge, Bel Bacio and La Lune Sucree. All of you are in this book, between the lines.

On a transreal basis, I am indebted to my college-era thesis triumvirate of troublemakers: Allen Strange, Rudy Rucker and Joel Slayton, each of whom delivered different dimensions of creative advice and surrogate-fatherly inspiration that induced me to start writing in the first place. Allow me to likewise give a nod to those academics who consoled me through all the frustrations of the current-day writer's life—Cathleen Miller and Alan Soldofsky, especially. And speaking of college, I must also thank three incredible women who put up with my soccer fandom in my twenties: Kimbel St. James, Yukiko Matsumoto and Kristina Naughton, each of whom taught me more than any college professor was ever able to do. Along with them came other roommates who also endured my soccer fandom: Scott Cofer, Garth Hurd, Mike Andrade (RIP), Patti Terando, Donna Fenton and Brian Hill.

Perhaps most importantly, thanks to everyone who ever played or worked for the San Jose Earthquakes, as well as their fans. You are part of history.

INTRODUCTION

In 1974, a group of athletes took to the streets of San Jose and guerrilla-marketed a new professional sport to an unknown city that was already in search of an identity. Their efforts helped vitalize the sport of soccer—not just in San Jose but across America as well. The initial crystallization of the San Jose Earthquakes lasted only ten years, but the aftershocks of their efforts reverberated across generations, resurfacing through multilayered lineages and leading straight up to the current-day activities of Major League Soccer. The contemporary San Jose Earthquakes carry on the historical narrative put into place by the original squad.

What follows is one author's experience with that historical narrative, almost from the very beginning. I grew up with the team in its original era and then evolved into a newspaper journalist decades later. As a result, I witnessed many of the plateaus and valleys, the successes and the heartbreaks, especially in modern-day times.

The story of the San Jose Earthquakes professional soccer club has unfolded as a microcosm of San Jose itself. It is a struggle for self-determination and acceptance against many higher-profile constituents. With a new era about to begin in a new permanent venue, Avaya Stadium, what follows here is a multilayered lasagna of historical trials and tribulations, all leading up to 2015. As with life, history often happens in cycles, so many characters tend to reappear at different moments throughout the continuum.

The Earthquakes never had an easy path or a simple process from point A to point B. It was a journey riddled with business potholes, periodic dearths of talent, absentee ownership groups and sheer fan heartbreak, seemingly over and over again. Even after two modern-day championships, worldwide superstars, team relocations and diehard fan support, there always seemed to be yet one more obstacle to overcome before any future, everlasting plans could finally materialize. Through it all, the Quakes and the sport have endured in San Jose—they will never say "die"—and now in 2015, the team has finally secured its first-ever permanent foundation in a brand-new stadium. Let history repeat.

CHAPTER 1

LATERAL SPREAD

From 1950 to 1969, Anthony P. "Dutch" Hamann managed the city of San Jose, California, during a time in which it transformed from a backwater fruit-packing cannery town into a vast horizontal amalgamation of manufacturing and residential subdivisions. By annexing over 1,300 pieces of land throughout his reign, Hamann and his policies helped increase San Jose's population from roughly 94,000 to 480,000, resulting in the textbook post–World War II suburban landscape still characterizing much of the city in 2015. To this day, Hamann's name continues to resurface as the policymaker who wanted San Jose to be "the Los Angeles of the North."

Regardless of San Jose's rapid population increase during those decades, the city operated underneath the umbrella of San Francisco, with residents and newspapermen of that more-famous city still viewing San Jose as the hinterland, the redheaded stepchild, a hick town or, as *San Francisco Chronicle* columnist Herb Caen wrote, "eleven freeway exits in search of a city." As San Jose grew, an attention-starved inferiority complex began to envelop the city like a blanket. Officials and many residents couldn't seem to discuss San Jose without contextualizing it against San Francisco, a complex that still bubbles to the surface of public policy and convention-business marketing to this day. During the 1960s, though, the identity complex was so ridiculous that, at one time, Santa Clara County's official tagline was "Only 45 minutes from San Francisco!" Seriously.

As Hamann's tenure barreled toward its conclusion, the more detrimental effects of his policies began to emerge. A once-thriving downtown descended into a black hole of empty buildings as big-box retail bailed for the suburbs. The city bulldozed historical structures and replaced them with empty parking lots. With the explosion of suburbia came new freeways, escalating traffic, en masse annihilation of orchards and ever-increasing citizen apathy. As horizontal growth spiraled out of control and cannibalized the hillsides, San Jose became a town in search of an identity.

None of this was lost on pop culture. Toward the end of Hamann's reign, in 1968, Dionne Warwick released "Do You Know the Way to San Jose?" a genteel yarn about a young country girl from San Jose who travels to LA and becomes disenchanted with the big city, only to return to her hometown, where "you can really breathe" and "they've got a lot of space." Warwick would later claim that San Joseans asked her to stop singing the song; they accused her of putting San Jose on the map and overpopulating it. In any event, the song became Warwick's biggest-selling tune and earned the singer her first Grammy Award.

Just as the aftermath of Hamann's policies reverberated into the early 1970s, the semiconductor industry was starting to explode throughout Santa Clara County. In 1971, journalist Don C. Hoefler was the first one to refer to the county as "Silicon Valley," in a series of articles for *Electronic News*. Researchers and academics were just beginning to implement the ARPANET, the predecessor to the Internet. Room-sized mainframe computers and punch cards were the norm.

On the radio, AM was king. FM's dominance was not even a figment in anyone's imagination. Television barely had any bands between 2, 4, 5, 7, 11 and 13. UHF had yet to emerge.

At the same time, in San Jose proper, citizens elected Norman Mineta as the first Asian American mayor of a major U.S. city. Mineta vowed to end once and for all the policies of suburban annexation and instead magnify the outreach from city hall into the now-sprawling neighborhoods, in order to give San Jose citizens a sense of identification.

Recalling those days in a 2014 conversation, the eighty-two-year-old Mineta told me what it was like back then. Forty years earlier, he had just wanted to give the town some civic pride. "No one knew were San Jose was," he said. "They may not have even known where Oakland was. But they knew the names San Diego, Sacramento, San Francisco. So we were sort of living under this shadow of these other communities. And I was trying to establish our own identity as a city."

As Mineta was trying to do exactly that, Major League Baseball's Oakland A's—located forty-five miles up the freeway, across the bay from San

Francisco—were in the midst of winning three consecutive World Series. The San Francisco 49ers of the NFL were into their first few seasons at Candlestick Park. By comparison, San Jose had no professional sports. The Bees, a single-A baseball squad, played at a four-thousand-capacity park located one mile south of San Jose State University and across the street from Spartan Stadium, the school's dilapidated football facility.

Activity-wise, over on the eastern edge of the city, a brand-spanking-new tri-level shopping complex, aptly titled Eastridge, had just opened with slaphappy, tippy-toe euphoria. At the time, it was the largest enclosed mall in the western United States. For families, though, San Jose's most popular destination was still Frontier Village, a folksy, Old West–themed amusement

San Jose mayor Norman Mineta and Krazy George, 1974. *George Henderson.*

park on a sunbaked highway in South San Jose surrounded by orchards. Those two locales, Eastridge and Frontier Village, were the highlights for kids in San Jose because there was nothing else to do.

ENTER SOCCERMAN

Into this entire theater of operations stepped Milan Mandaric, a self-made electronics entrepreneur and passionate soccer fan from a country then called Yugoslavia. After immigrating to the Bay Area in the late 1960s, Mandaric founded his own printed circuit-board business, Lika Corporation, and hit the big time in Santa Clara County just as San Jose, the former Prune Capital of the World, was experiencing unprecedented growth. In his early thirties, Mandaric was already a wealthy man living in the nearby posh hamlet of Saratoga with a tennis court in his backyard.

Just about the time Mandaric was transplanting to the United States, two fledgling soccer mini-leagues joined together and formed the North American Soccer League (NASL), which began play in 1968. One of the previous mini-leagues, the National Professional Soccer League, featured the Oakland Clippers, a team dominated by players from Yugoslavia. The team joined the new NASL, but the first few seasons of the NASL did not catch on enough for the league to sustain itself. The Clippers folded after the inaugural 1968 season, and the league as a whole imploded from seventeen teams to five—not exactly a good sign.

As the NASL slowly began figuring out how to reinvent itself, league commissioner Phil Woosnam and president Lamar Hunt began to strategize how the NASL could once again flourish on the West Coast. They came up with successful schemes for Seattle, Vancouver and Los Angeles. Their fourth location needed to be the San Francisco Bay Area.

Mandaric had already lurked in the shadows of the Clippers' demise, befriending the Slavs and making friends throughout the Bay Area soccer community. When he got wind of the NASL's plans to return to the San Francisco Bay Area, he established a network of correspondence and organized a potential squad, mostly of ex-Clipper folk and players from local amateur leagues.

Instead of becoming the third professional sports franchise in San Francisco or Oakland, Mandaric wanted to start the first-ever pro team in San Jose. As a result, in 1973, Woosnam and Hunt came to San Jose to meet

Momcilo "Gabbo" Gavric playing for the Oakland Clippers. *History San Jose.*

with Mandaric and discuss his interest in owning a new NASL franchise. The first of many heated territorial discussions began to unfold.

In a now-legendary series of arguments that extended into 1974, Hunt and Woosnam insisted that any new Bay Area franchise of the NASL be located, or at least named, after San Francisco. They considered San Jose to be a hick town with no "there" there and initially dismissed any idea to name a team after the former Prune Capital of the World. Dionne Warwick would have been proud.

View of downtown San Jose, 1974. *History San Jose.*

San Jose Mercury reporter Fred Guzman, who went on to cover the team for the rest of the 1970s, chronicled these discussions for that newspaper. Even after Mandaric was awarded the franchise in late 1973; even after Mandaric declared on January 16, 1974, that San Jose would host the team, with the NASL expansion draft beginning a week later; and even after the 1974 season schedule was already written, Hunt, Woosnam and league officials still refused to accept a team named after San Jose. They would not budge, insisting on San Francisco due to its higher celebrity status.

In a February 4, 1974 *San Jose Mercury* piece titled "Sour Notes Emerging from NASL," Guzman led his story with Dionne Warwick. "Maybe it's simply a matter of musical tastes," Guzman wrote. "A great number of people, after all, favor Tony Bennett's rendition of 'I Left My Heart in San Francisco' over Dionne Warwick's 'Do You Know the Way to San Jose?'"

Four days later, Mandaric flew off to Toronto for an official league meeting to convince everyone else that San Jose would indeed be a hotbed for soccer. His new master of promotions, Dick Berg, went with him.

PROMOTIONAL MASTER

When Milan Mandaric initially announced on January 16, 1974, that San Jose would host a new NASL franchise, he also announced that Dick Berg would be the team's general manager. Mandaric was thirty-five years old, Berg, thirty. Originally a Stanford quarterback, Berg had worked for the Seattle SuperSonics NBA franchise during that team's initial stages before spending four years as the promotions director for the San Francisco 49ers, where he ratcheted up the game experience with zany halftime shows and celebrity appearances. He specialized in unusual promotional tactics and stunts to help cement a sport's place in the consciousness of the general public. It was Berg, for instance, who helped orchestrate a Lou Rawls performance of the national anthem at a 49ers game, after which Rawls then helicoptered across the bay to the Oakland airport in order to sing it again twenty minutes later at an Oakland A's World Series game, after which he helicoptered right back to ride an elephant at halftime.

As a result of Berg's wacky ways, the Niners' attendance figures had practically doubled under his four-year tenure. This is the same time frame that saw the Niners move from Kezar Stadium into the much more modern and freeway-accessible Candlestick Park, at the southern expanses of San Francisco. It was Berg who helped convince the 49ers' management to fully realize the potential of a fan base hailing predominantly from the South Bay and the Peninsula, rather than San Francisco proper.

As a result, both Berg and Mandaric were primed to launch San Jose's first-ever professional sports franchise. Upon the announcement declaring San Jose the team's home and Berg the GM, Fred Guzman led his story with: "San Jose has finally become a major-league city." He quoted mayor Norman Mineta as saying there was probably a strong interest in soccer in San Jose due to the very large Portuguese and Mexican American communities.

In San Jose, Mandaric declared Spartan Stadium at San Jose State University as the new team's home. Spartan was an aging facility at best, and seemingly endless schemes to expand it from seventeen thousand seats to over thirty thousand were already on the drawing board. As a contingency plan, Mandaric said he would not rule out Buck Shaw Stadium at nearby Santa Clara University, should construction commence at Spartan.

San Francisco newspapermen were not giddy about a new sport emerging in the hinterland. Legendary *Chronicle* columnist Herb Caen wrote that Dick Berg had left the 49ers to "sink with soccer in San Jose." The ever-eloquent *Chronicle* sports editor Art Rosenbaum was equally skeptical, claiming that better amateur soccer was already played every weekend at Balboa Stadium in San Francisco and that San Jose fans, at the very least, deserved a decent product on the field.

The original 1974 San Jose Earthquakes. *History San Jose.*

However, the NASL executives, especially co-founder Lamar Hunt, still firmly insisted that any new team in the Bay Area be named after San Francisco, not San Jose—which meant that Mandaric and Berg were not done with the fight. Hunt invited the two of them to a league meeting in Toronto to discuss the matter. On February 8, 1974, Berg and Mandaric attended the meeting to convince the NASL and team officials that San Jose deserved its first major-league team.

"The league meeting was all about us," Berg recalled. "They had about twelve of the teams stand up and say, 'No, it has to be San Francisco.' And finally they called on me, and I gave them all I could possibly muster as far as the passion I had and the background I had that San Francisco was simply 'a losing place for y'all, and if that's going to be your choice, then good luck with it and I won't be involved.' And Mr. Mandaric got up and said, 'I, too, will not be involved.'"

According to Berg's recollection of the events, Commissioner Woosnam then stopped the meeting and asked Berg and Mandaric to temporarily leave the room while the others discussed it. Hunt then came out to ask the two of them for details in private, with Berg and Mandaric repeating their arguments and standing their ground. Berg and Mandaric insisted on San

Jose or nowhere. That was their position. The league could take it or leave it. Hunt then went back into the meeting, and a few moments unfolded before Berg and Mandaric were asked to come back inside.

As Berg remembers it: "The commissioner said, 'Mr. Mandaric and Mr. Berg, would you please stand up?' And we said okay, figuring our next step was out the door. And he said, 'We've had a vote. And the vote was 14–1. They want you in the league.'"

And that is how the San Jose Earthquakes went legit.

"I can almost cry about it now, it was so exciting," Berg recalled. "Because we really felt like they were just not going to take it."

As a result, that hick town in the hinterland now had its first-ever major-league sports franchise.

CHAPTER 2

GROUND MOTION

As the franchise got off the ground, Berg unleashed a grand, unprecedented plan to saturate the general San Jose public with player appearances and create an environment where all the fans could get to know the team personally. To Berg, person-to-person interaction was better than anything print advertising could accomplish. Selling a new team in a new sport for the first time in a city's history required massive eyeball-to-eyeball promotion. Each person whom a player met on the street, anywhere, was a potential new fan. It was guerrilla marketing before the term was even invented. Berg had excelled at such tactics in both Seattle and San Francisco, and he was primed and ready to put San Jose on the major-league sports map.

As a result, the San Jose Earthquakes operated on two fronts: on the field itself and on the streets to spread the gospel of the game. At least in the first several seasons, the team operated as a family unit, partying with the fans and hanging out with one another in public. There was really no separation between fighting for one another on the pitch and selling the game to the San Jose populace. All fans were considered part of the family, and many fans at every single game had already met one of the players ahead of time. Such an approach was unheard of in pro sports at that time.

Those first few squads either reached the playoffs or, in one case, even won an indoor soccer championship. The stars were aplenty those first few years, but folks like Paul Child, Mani Hernandez, Johnny Moore, Gabbo

Gavric, Art Welch, Mirko Stojanovich, Archie Roboostoff and the Demling brothers, Mark and Buzz, plus many more, all paved the way for what was to evolve decades later.

Scottish expat Johnny Moore, then twenty-six, came on board as a player and assistant general manager. Moore and Berg essentially started the club's front office in the old San Jose Hyatt Hotel on North First Street. Berg was the conductor, and Moore's job was to take it to the streets. As a result, every other player was required to go along with the plan. Everyone had to do public speaking engagements, parties, school visits and other events—all to help the sell the game. Players often did three to four appearances a day.

"It was like a startup, if you equate it to the electronics industry," said original Quake Davie Kemp, a Scotsman who went on to launch a company in Silicon Valley. "It's a startup. Nobody knows about it, you have to get your name out there and the people who are involved in it are excited about it. They want to be part of it."

Birmingham, England native Paul Child originally played for Atlanta in 1972 and 1973 but went back to England to live in his parents' house when the Atlanta franchise folded after the 1973 season. After he came to play for San Jose's inaugural team at age twenty-one, Child went on to become the NASL's leading scorer that year and remained San Jose's star forward for the rest of the 1970s.

Upon Child's arrival in San Jose, he was key in the guerrilla marketing strategy. For him, it was culture shock. When previously playing for Atlanta or back in England, interacting

The Scotsmen of the 1975 San Jose Earthquakes. *From left to right*: Johnny Moore, Jimmy Johnstone and Davie Kemp. *History San Jose.*

The San Jose Earthquakes winning the 1975 NASL indoor championship. *History San Jose.*

with the general public had not been part of Child's job. Now in San Jose, they were taking him to appearances at car dealerships and making him juggle soccer balls at shopping centers. He visited people's homes for dinner, attended youth soccer practices and delivered lectures at the Elks Lodge. "As soon as I got there and I signed, Dick Berg took me to every Kiwanis Club, every Boy Scout meeting, every practice," Child recalled. "I went to the 49ers banquets with him and just everywhere. I was out every night. They were promoting me as one of the top players in the league and coming into San Jose. Then I had to start thinking, 'Boy, I'd better be good.'"

Launching the first-ever pro sports franchise in a completely unknown city proved to be inspiring. What an opportunity. "That's what made it a little bit different," Child said. "Where a team has already been established, and players come in, there's always those hardcore guys that are there, and you're thinking, 'Are they going to accept me or are they not going to accept me?'"

The feeling among players that the team was a family unit, both on and off the field, is what made it all succeed in those early years, recalled Moore in a 2014 conversation: "The chance to be the first team ever in San Jose—the guys understood that, so they became very, very tight. We'd have a drink on a Tuesday or Wednesday night…we had eighteen players, so there'd be eighteen of us there. We didn't go crazy, but everybody was part of it. If you missed it, that wasn't cool. And we built a real close relationship, and that helped make the whole thing work."

And when the team hit the streets to sell the sport to a brand-new audience, it was Berg who orchestrated much of the grand scheme. The players made themselves visible everywhere and accessible to everyone. "We went anywhere," Moore said. "If someone called and said, 'My son's having a birthday party,' one of the guys would say, 'Yeah, I'll go.' Go to their house, shake hands with the kids, get their picture taken. And then that family was at the game."

Paul Child promotional card, 1974. *History San Jose.*

And that family often came back to the games. The team maintained relationships with its people from there on out. It was a brilliant marketing strategy. "It became even more important once they became fans," Moore said. "We never backed off. If anybody called, we were there."

San Jose native John Jussen grew up with the Quakes, starting from the very first game. His parents, who had emigrated directly from Holland, enjoyed hanging out with the team, a phenomenon they'd not seen in Europe. "We'd go on the field after the game and talk to the players," Jussen recalled. "And it was a big deal. They got to know my mom pretty well. [Quakes defender] Laurie Calloway came over to our house for dinner with his wife, a big deal for a ten-year-old kid. I remember thinking, 'Oh my god, Laurie Calloway's at my house!'"

Countless others who grew up in San Jose during the 1970s have similar stories: "Paul Child came to my house for dinner," "Easy Perez came to my practice," "Johnny Moore came to my school" or "We used to watch them practice and go collect all the balls."

San Jose Earthquakes Shakers greeting Kyle Rote Jr. at the San Francisco Airport, 1975. *Debbie Hilpert.*

Dick Berg also devised a new type of trading card as a promotional gimmick: a nine-inch circular card shaped like a soccer ball that each player distributed to the general public. The players carried their own cards wherever they went and autographed them for anyone who asked. "Every guy had like a thousand of those," recalled Mark Demling, the Quakes' vocal defender and first-ever draft pick. "And you'd put fifty to one hundred in your bag. And so after the game, if somebody wanted your autograph, you pulled out your card and you signed your card. And you gave it to the kid, and the kids would have a collection of them up on their wall, of all the guys. Instead of signing a piece of paper, it'd be like Stan Musial having his own baseball cards and signing his card."

The circular cards featured the players' stats, height, weight, hometown and other pertinent information. According to Demling, the stunt caught on like wildfire. "People started doing that all around the league because the players would come here and see us with these things and signing them, and they thought they were really cool," Demling said.

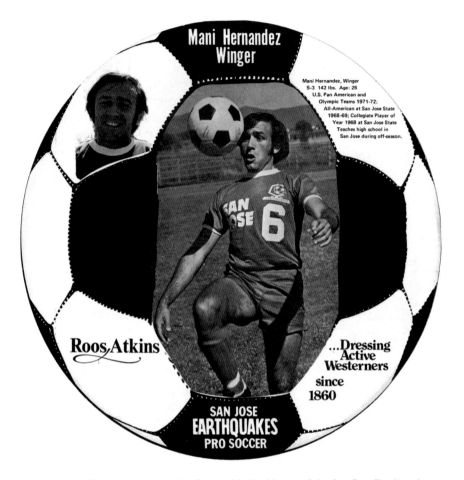

Forward Mani Hernandez scored the first goal in the history of the San Jose Earthquakes. *History San Jose.*

Dave "Obie" Obenour was the second trainer at De Anza College after that institution opened in the late 1960s. He signed on to be the Earthquakes' inaugural trainer in 1974, a position he kept for the rest of that decade. "Trainer" was a more ambiguous term in those days, so Obie drove buses, orchestrated meals, booked travel arrangements and became part of the family. In a 2014 conversation, he said that back in those days, the variety of ethnicities in the club is what touched him the deepest.

"It was the diversity," Obenour said. "Meeting the British, meeting the local guys, meeting the Serbians, meeting these different players from all over the world. And them confiding in me on injury issues."

And since everyone hung out with everyone else off the field as well, in many cases, the British players learned about Mexican food, something they'd never seen, and the Americans learned about British food when going to dinner at the local homes of British players. It was a cross-cultural exchange through the language of San Jose soccer.

"It made me a more dynamic person," Obenour said. "And my family as well. My two boys both played soccer, and it instilled a lot [in them]. And like a lot of the American guys, their kids all grew up loving the game of soccer. Before that, soccer was so-so—it was more of an ethnic sport. And after [the emergence of the Earthquakes], you saw punks and kids playing all the time, you know?"

However, a brand-new team taking to the streets to sell what some natives considered a "foreign" sport and what daily newspaper editors considered a "commie sport" required more than just the players. It required cheerleaders. In San Jose, they were called the Shakers, and they attended all the promotional appearances with the players, including lunches, radio spots and shopping mall stunts at Eastridge Mall, which had opened just a few years earlier.

Berg orchestrated the Shaker strategy, expanding on what he'd already accomplished with the 49ers. While with the Niners, decades before social media, Berg had organized the "Niner Nuggets," a band of promotional women who took to the streets and traveled far into the suburbs—all the way to San Jose—to hype the 49ers via various public promotional appearances. The San Jose Earthquakes Shakers amplified the concept even more. Decked out in cardinal-red skirts and wide-brimmed hats, they accompanied the players to every promo.

"They went everywhere with us," Demling said. "They did so many promotions, just like the guys. We used to juggle in the foyer [at Eastridge], and while we were juggling, the girls were on the second and third floors handing out information on tickets or who we were playing that week. Seriously, it wasn't a joke; we were doing all this stuff that was in *Slap Shot*. In *Slap Shot*, when they had the fashion show…we were doing fashion shows."

None of the players had any idea how long it was going to last. They just wanted to spread the gospel of soccer to a new city that was experiencing its first major-league sport.

"I couldn't think, 'Is this team going to be around after a year?'" Child said. "'Are they going to fold? Are they going to run out of money? Are no people going to come to the games?' You come with all those thoughts flying through your head. All you hope is, 'Boy, I hope we can make this really work

A San Jose Earthquakes Shaker handing out promotional materials. *History San Jose.*

Johnny Moore signing autographs. *History San Jose.*

because it's our future as well as San Jose's future, for the fans and everything.' I just think we had a group of guys that wanted to do that because we went and did anything we could do to preach the word of soccer."

Former *San Jose Mercury* reporter Fred Guzman agreed. In 2009, I was working on a cover story for *Metro Silicon Valley*, San Jose's alternative weekly newspaper, when I called him on the phone. As he recalled those seasons, Guzman said that the Earthquakes had limitations as a soccer team, but they succeeded at selling the game to unprecedented degrees. "The players may not have been world class in talent, but they bought into that marketing game plan and executed it to perfection," he told me. "It was almost like they were on a crusade for their sport. They conducted clinics all over the Bay Area, they signed autographs until they got writer's cramp, they attended the post-game parties, they wore the sweat-tops in public—a pro in another place wouldn't do that; he'd wear an Armani, you know?"

CHAPTER 3

THE EPICENTER

Although technically the home turf of San Jose State University's football team, Spartan Stadium was located one mile south of the main campus. Built on a dirt hill in 1933 with a capacity of six thousand, Spartan Stadium had expanded over the decades to approximately seventeen thousand. But by the time the early 1970s rolled around, it was showing its age in dramatic fashion. Before the Earthquakes began their inaugural season, college football and graduation ceremonies made up the majority of Spartan Stadium's use. There were no chairs, only wooden benches. Two dilapidated media boxes, in faded Spartan yellow, sat atop the grandstands on either side of the stadium. The locker rooms sat at the north end of the stadium, and players entered the pitch from an ancient asphalt ramp that took them down to the field from the lockers. Throughout the grounds, only a few scattered restroom facilities existed, along with rickety wooden maintenance offices. Trees covered the grounds, giving the property an old-school campus kind of feel.

Spartan had plodded on through the times, but with the city's population escalating and its geographical sprawl ever increasing, university officials, SJSU football fans and politicians alike were grumbling for a larger venue to reflect a more prideful city. The humble, downtrodden stadium was simply too small for a team with higher NCAA conference ambitions. Even as early as the late 1960s, schemes to expand Spartan Stadium began to hit the boardrooms.

But none of this stopped the San Jose Earthquakes. They were there to build a professional expansion franchise from the bottom up and sell a new sport to families all over San Jose.

Quakes lining up to play the California Surf, 1978. *Dave Obenour.*

"The players were so pumped about being part of it that we never negatively saw Spartan Stadium," Moore recalled. "We saw it as a real positive, honestly. The locker rooms were old, but that was the least of our problems. The field was tight, but that was the least of our problems. We had crowds, we had excitement and we got paid to play. Everyone was pumped."

At the time, most American football fields were roughly fifty yards wide, much narrower than soccer pitches, and many stadiums were built to accommodate NFL crowds in the tens of thousands. In those venues, plenty of room existed on the sidelines, between the crowds and the field. The fans seemed nowhere near the players. As the North American Soccer League went through its initial ups and downs through the early 1970s, the franchises that shared facilities with NFL squads often played in lonely, dismal environments, drawing four-figure attendance numbers in cavernous, empty stadiums. It did not bode well for the intimate fan experience.

But when the Earthquakes began play, Spartan became the exception. At fifty yards wide and one hundred yards long, the pitch was ridiculously small for soccer, and there was barely any room on the sidelines for the players to take corner kicks. Cement barriers just a few yards from the sidelines were all that separated the crowds from the players on the pitch. As a result, the fans were unusually close to the action, and the overall tight confines enabled the crowd to be almost on top of the players. Even from several rows up, one could hear the players talking to one another on the field, see the scrapes on their shins, follow their spit hitting the ground or, if one occupied the front row, even lean over the railing and verbally taunt the visiting team's bench within a few feet of their ears.

All of this played a significant role in Spartan becoming the most heralded home turf in the league during the Quakes' first two seasons, when they led the NASL in home attendance. Before 1974, just about every other team in the league had averaged four-figure attendances since the league's inception, but the Quakes averaged 16,584 in 1974 and 17,927 in 1975. Other teams eventually demolished those numbers, but this was during a time when the New York Cosmos still played on Randall's Island, before the Pelé phenomenon had reached its glitz and glamour and before the dramatic excess of the Cosmos had exploded. Until the Earthquakes started, no team in the NASL had regularly drawn anything near 17,000 people a match. Oddly enough, 17,000 at that time was more than what the San Francisco Giants or the Oakland A's were averaging, even though the latter team had just won the World Series three years in a row.

The tiny, dilapidated Spartan Stadium thus offered an environment unlike any other facility in the league. To many of the foreign-born players, either with the Quakes or on opposing teams, the tight confines of screaming attendees added a much-needed authenticity to matches, authenticity not found at other NASL venues. "Suddenly, every player in the league wanted to play here," Moore recalled. "Guys that would come in and see it crowded and noisy—the European guys, the South American guys—they felt like, 'Hey, this is the way it's supposed to be. It's like back home. This is the game; this is the noise.' At Spartan, more than any other stadium in the league, it fit that mold."

The jammed environment was so refreshing that even former mayor Norman Mineta has memories of attending matches when the Quakes first started. He said the diversity of his hometown folk brought a joyous feeling to his heart, although there was some backlash against what some considered a "commie sport," a sport for immigrants or a sport that attracted "those people."

"I remember going to the games at San Jose State, Spartan Stadium, and hearing languages in the stadium, different languages. To me, that was just terrific," Mineta told me. "So that's what I wanted to encourage. But I think there were a lot of people who were still of the mind of resisting stuff to help the Earthquakes because it brought in 'those kinds of people.'"

The intimate, jam-packed stands and the noise that came along with them tended to submerge opposing teams, but that wasn't all. The compact, postage stamp size of the Spartan Stadium pitch also became an asset. The lack of wide expanses from sideline to sideline to which players were normally accustomed became a unique home-turf advantage for the Earthquakes. There was no space for opposing midfielders to adequately distribute the ball, defenders barely had any ability to build from the back and many instances in which players could open up spaces were essentially nullified.

Even better, the Earthquakes were a gritty, working-class ilk who, despite their lack of world-beating prowess, took advantage of the narrow confines to confront any possible attack in near-belligerent fashion, often overwhelming a visiting squad. Plus, the capacity crowd became the best twelfth man anywhere in North America.

"The team…it had major limitations as a soccer team, but…Spartan Stadium was so narrow—even narrower than it is now—you would put these guys out there, and the crowd would start going crazy and these players would just come at you," Guzman told me. "I mean, they were tough, aggressive and unrelenting, so they were playing with almost like a full-court press in this little bandbox," he said. "The place was so narrow, and you couldn't get away from them. And all of a sudden, the crowd was on top of you. The people were screaming…it was a tremendous environment. So the quality of the soccer in such a small, little place might not be the most elegant in the world, but man, it was intense."

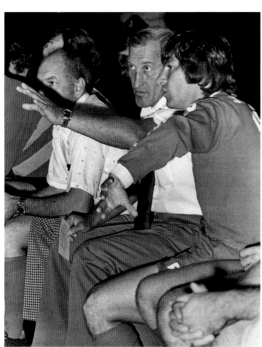

Head coach Ivan Toplak and Johnny Moore overseeing the action. *History San Jose.*

For the fans, interaction with the players on game day began at the tailgate parties, which usually unfolded on the grass at the east side of Spartan Stadium. The players were actually required to go over and meet the families hanging out before the game, a practice unheard of in professional sports at the time.

"We used to go to Los Gatos Lodge for a pre-game meal before going to the stadium," Moore recalled. "And at Spartan, the deal was, don't just park your car and walk into the locker room. Park your car, walk around and say hello before you come in."

Some players even came back to the tailgate area after the match just to drink and eat with the fans. It was all one big party, with a variety of ethnicities making the food offerings more than worthwhile. The players had access to a veritable smorgasbord of beers and grub. For the mid-1970s, such a scenario was way ahead of its time. The tailgates at Earthquakes games might have been the first bona fide public international food courts in the entire San Francisco Bay Area. "There was always plenty to eat," Demling said. "There were Mexican people, where you'd get all the beers like Dos Equis or Tecate, and you'd get a taco. And then you'd go over and see some German guy a few rows over, and you'd get a Beck's and a bratwurst or something. We played a lot of games in the afternoon, and you could just literally walk around the parking lot." Moore added, "Some of the guys, that was the best they ate all week. Some of the college guys...they weren't making a lot of money."

The Quakes' booster club, known as the Aftershocks, organized grand-scale after parties that often unfolded at a local hotel or Lou's Village, a legendary local restaurant and banquet facility. All fans were welcome. "Someone always bought you a beer," Demling said.

For the fans, many of us being little kids at the time, the tailgating was just the beginning of the experience. Once inside the stadium, fans crammed in tight and came up with a term, "Pack the Pit," to describe the tight confines. The more rambunctious, unruly and hyperactive kids who couldn't sit still devised their own activities. I recall sliding down the dirt hill behind the eastern grandstand on a flattened cardboard box. For many kids, this activity was a part of the gameday experience, especially during halftime. We'd rifle through empty boxes discarded by the concession stands and then carry the boxes up to the top of the eastern grandstand. After stepping over the railing to get behind the benches, we'd proceed to slide down the dirt hill, toboggan-style, to the cement concourse below, occasionally crashing into a tree in the process.

Running around at Spartan Stadium in those days proved to be easy. Some of us even played hide-and-seek in the myriad trees throughout the grounds, usually to the explosive annoyance of our parents.

Since barely any semblance of security existed, I recall running down the ramp to the pitch and standing behind the goal, during the game, and

Quakes players at Spartan Stadium, 1974. *From left to right*: Johnny Moore, Archie Roboostoff and Boris Bandov. *Dave Obenour.*

catching the errant shots at age ten. As long as I didn't abuse the situation, no one seemed to care. I would even go out of my way to get on the post-game TV cameras—anything to drag out the experience. I never wanted to leave.

San Jose's Buzz Demling fights off Malcolm Linton of the Los Angeles Aztecs. *History San Jose.*

Back in those days, Spartan Stadium also allowed fans to bring their own beer into the stadium. After the game concluded, it was common for some of us kids to walk around in the stands with plastic garbage bags and pick up the leftover beer cans, just to recycle them afterward.

Jussen recalls this same scenario. Quakes matches taught him how to recycle, how to work for his money. He learned how to be a businessman. "We'd bring Hefty bags, my brother and I, and we'd pick up all the beer cans until late," Jussen recalled. "I think we got about thirteen dollars every game from collecting the cans, so it was a pretty big deal even back then—a lot of money. And the ticket was six dollars to get in."

Since Spartan did, indeed, allow beer, fans often lugged in their own ice chests. In one case, it led to an incident that people still talk about to this day:

the infamous Willie Johnston beer swig goal of 1979. On one particular night, during what eventually became their championship season, the Vancouver Whitecaps rolled into Spartan Stadium for a match. With the game tied 1–1, Johnston, a former Glasgow Rangers legend, nabbed a swig from a fan's beer before taking a corner kick for the Whitecaps. As Johnston carried the ball to the corner flag in preparation for the kick, twenty-four-year-old Frank Smillie leaned over the cement barrier, beer in hand. Johnston motioned, the bottle exchanged hands and Willie took a swig. The corner kick then led directly to a goal. A YouTube video of the play still exists and gets regular views whenever the current Whitecaps come to San Jose.

Addressing the Public

As the fans went wild every game, along with the city's debut professional sports franchise came its own unique staff, many of whom also pioneered their respective techniques, primarily because there was no rulebook, no blueprint and no guidelines for how any of this was to be done. The characters behind the microphones proved to be no exception.

For practically the whole decade of the 1970s, Bob Ray was the morning drive guy on KLIV, at that time a local AM rock station. When the Earthquakes asked him to be their public address announcer for the games at Spartan Stadium, he used his talents for radio theatrics to transform a mere game into an experiential event for the fans. For one, Ray devised unique ways of announcing each player's name. Archie Roboostoff became "Archie RrrrrrrrrrrrrrrrrrrrrrrROBoostoff!" Ray seemed to exhibit just as much passion for his craft as did the players. There were no dulcet tones emerging from the press box.

Ray recently met me at Britannia Arms, a local British pub, and I asked him if anyone else at that time was implementing those types of sports announcing techniques. In theatrical fashion, he said no. "There was nobody doing anything, except for some very wonderfully talented voices, but just voices doing standard announcements of names and numbers and substitutions," said Ray. "I decided that wasn't going to work for me. I wanted to make it exciting, so when I introduced Archie Roboostoff one day, I just rolled the Rs because I'm fluent in Spanish, and it caught on."

Hearing Ray's antics at the game was exactly like listening to a radio DJ doing his shtick, but from the press box instead, which completely enhanced

Pre-game festivities at Spartan Stadium, 1978. *Dave Obenour.*

the fan experience. If someone left his or her car running in the parking lot, or if a small child strayed from his parents, the game staff alerted Ray, who then developed poignant but humorous storytelling skits to announce the details for the entire stadium to hear.

"Information would come in about lost children," Ray recalled. "And I'd make a little story out of it. I would say, 'You know little Johnny went out to buy some popcorn, and Mr. and Mrs. Chris, do you know where little Johnny is now? He's with his popcorn looking for you by aisle twenty-five.' People would laugh, and it worked into the matrix of the experience."

As he continued to reflect on those days, Ray was visibly moved by his own recollections of how much the Earthquakes' original era meant to him, then a young whippersnapper radio guy in his twenties, someone just trying to upset the applecart of boring, sedate DJs. The Quakes players became like family to him. "I had no idea of how much it would absorb my life," he confessed. "I met a group of kids—kids in that some of them were a little younger than me at that particular time—who were passionate about this game, and as I learned it, I infused my style of announcing, which was not staid and reserved, into the game."

Even though all of this felt brand new to those involved, the uniqueness of the San Jose Earthquakes experience at Spartan Stadium did not stop there. The home-turf advantage of a city's first major pro sport was just the beginning. For certain, a group of working-class players and their coaches and staff, along with newbie fan enthusiasm directed toward the opposing squads, contributed to the environment. But to lift the entire circus to unprecedented heights required one final human component. It took a very specific kind of perpetrator—not a cheerleader, but an instigator—an obnoxious, flamboyant troublemaker to stir up the emotions of sixteen thousand people using only a snare drum and his own gravelly voice.

CHAPTER 4
GOING STIR KRAZY

Krazy George Henderson attended what was then called San Jose State College in the mid- to late 1960s and began to volunteer as a cheerleader in the stands at Spartan football games. At the time, when silly synchronized dancing and cheering dominated college sports and the guys were required to wear frat-boy sweaters, Henderson had other things in mind. He grabbed a snare drum and took his act into the stands.

At San Jose State, no other cheerleader would venture into the actual seats in order to rouse the fans' passions and voices. George was the first. His ambitions led him to cheerlead/instigate on behalf of the Oakland Seals hockey team for a few seasons, where he famously egged on a visiting Boston Bruins team to nearly attack him by scaling the glass.

When the Earthquakes began play in 1974, George was teaching electronics at nearby Buchser High School. Dick Berg brought him on board and paid him thirty-five dollars a game to instigate mass cheers, ridicule the opposing players and, most notably, stage grand-scale entrances before each kickoff. For example, just before kickoff at the very first Earthquakes game in May 1974, an ambulance suddenly entered the field and drove straight to the team's bench. Everyone in the stands thought a player was already hurt. But lo and behold, Krazy George then popped out of the ambulance—game ball in one hand, snare drum in the other—to officially declare that the match was about to begin.

From then on, Berg and Krazy George plotted an endless variety of zany ways that George could enter the field at the beginning of the match: in a garbage truck, police car or limousine; from a helicopter or hang glider; or even on the back of a camel. As a result, George became an integral component of the gameday experience. Fans made sure to be in their seats by kickoff because everyone wanted to see what George would do next. He initiated the crowd into the experience from the very beginning. And once the game started, there he was in the stands, beating his snare drum, standing on the top of the visiting team's box, leading sixteen thousand people in mass cheers and insulting all of the visiting players during the game. No one in any professional sport had seen any such thing. It was pure theater.

"The component that he added, just from a technical side, was to bring the crowd into the game immediately," Ray said. "Soccer can have its back-and-forth, which is one of the issues that still plagues the game to this day with an American audience—the back-and-forth lack of scoring in some cases. George was out there banging that drum from the beginning, and the crowd loved him. Loved him."

This was the very beginning of Krazy George's professional career, and he went on to rouse fans at baseball, football and hockey games, plus the World Cup and the Olympics. Of course, he also unarguably invented "the wave" years later. But back then, he was an integral part of the Earthquakes experience.

"You weren't going to 'just the game,'" said Ray. "There was so much more that was going on there, so much more—especially in the beginning."

At current San Jose Earthquakes home matches in MLS, when fans implement the back-and-forth "EARTH!/QUAKES!" cheer, with respective sides of the stadium alternating each word over and over again, it's the exact same cheer Krazy George invented in 1974. Even today, his influence lives on.

Mark Demling recalls hearing those cheers from the field as a player in the 1970s. Even from the pitch, the cheers were unreal. "I can remember one game…honestly, I think it went on for five minutes," Demling recalled. "He just kept going. And the crowd kept going. Right in the middle of the game. EARTH! QUAKES! EARTH! QUAKES! It was crazy. I mean, it literally was crazy. It was wild."

To get sixteen thousand people, game after game, all screaming the same thing was not a regular experience in those days. In retrospect, the whole package felt like a stadium rock show for those of us who were kids. There was a certain rumble, a thunderous vibe as we entered the stadium, as we sat down and as we waited in anticipation for George to enter the field.

As Henderson explained it to me in 2014, Dick Berg orchestrated the fan interaction from the very beginning. A passive audience simply wasn't allowed. "I think most pro sports at that time were viewed as: if you went

A young Krazy George at Spartan Stadium. *Dave Obenour.*

to the game, you didn't have to cheer, as in college sports," Henderson said. "You paid the extra money to make them win, and they got paid to win. So you really didn't have to support them and be behind them as much. But that was the difference with Dick Berg. He said, 'I want the fans involved in the game.' And that's what I did."

Part of George's shtick was to insult the visiting team as much as it could tolerate. Since Dick Berg still had connections, he often incorporated animals in specific stunts that no one could possibly get away with nowadays. For example, Seattle Sounders goalkeeper Barry Walting used to keep two teddy bears in his goal for good luck. So the Quakes used their connections to secure two real bears. When George entered the field, he brought the two bears and ran with them in front of Walting, just for a joke. In other instances, the visiting team would come down the ramp, only to see a tiger sitting there to greet them, as if the tiger was the security guard.

The vibe continued throughout the game, with everyone anticipating where in the stands George and his drum would emerge next. And in the stands, one felt directly connected to the game and the experience both as a contributor and a participant, not just a static audience member. To heist concepts from quantum mechanics, we were part of the experiment, not separate observers. Every component of the experience—George and the fans, the trees hanging overhead, the rotten bathrooms, the ice chests, the impromptu self-directed kids' adventures throughout the stadium and the bored security guards—affected everything else. It was all connected, all one giant breathing, conscious organism. No other pro sport offered any such thing at that time. George tied it all together.

And the timing was perfect. San Jose was ready for its first major-league sport, and everyone was ready to ignore rules and regulations to make it happen. To this day, no one seems to know how many of the stunts were legal or not.

"I don't know how many times they brought George in on a helicopter," Ray recalled. "They landed a helicopter in the middle of Spartan Stadium. No matter who you talk to, there were no permits. No, no, they just landed a helicopter. You couldn't do that today. There's absolutely no way the FAA is going to allow a helicopter to fly over and land inside Spartan Stadium and let George come out of it."

When talking to me for a *Metro Silicon Valley* story in 2009, Guzman emphasized that Krazy George pioneered an entirely new component of the professional sports experience. There was no previous frame of reference. "That stuff was considered bush league—you know, having all this loud, garish music and Krazy George leading people in mass cheers," Guzman said. "[Now] that's all become customary in professional sports, but it was rather unique then. In a baseball game, you just showed up, they said 'play ball,' you played and then you went home. So a lot of the things that [the Earthquakes] did, like giveaways and all this other stuff, were really rather unique for the time."

Krazy George entering the field in yet another zany fashion. *History San Jose.*

With the utmost humility, Bob Ray, whose advertising agency helped orchestrate some of the giveaways and gimmicks, agreed. He even went as far as to say that the Quakes wrote the book on how to transform a sport into an experiential event. Ray suggested that much of what goes on in other sports today is directly inherited from the hysteria that went down in Spartan Stadium forty years ago. "The marketing in soccer became the blueprint, I think, for many things that are going on today, including what's going on at AT&T Park, where they've taken the park itself and also the experience of going to AT&T Park," said Ray. "That's great. I understand that. I'm very happy for them, but the [experiential aspect] of going to a sports event started with the San Jose Earthquakes. It started with the North American Soccer League, and it started right here with that game, Krazy George and all the shenanigans that we could dream of to entertain people."

CHAPTER 5

PELÉ, BESTIE AND THE GODS

M any of the world's greatest players came to play in the NASL. Some of these godlike figures were past their primes, but others came at the height of their careers. Legends like Franz Beckenbauer, Johan Cruyff, Gerd Mueller, Eusebio, Bobby Moore, George Best and countless others gave fans and other NASL players the chance to experience football royalty from around the globe. In other cases, players like Peter Beardsley came to the NASL at a very young age before returning to Europe and moving on to heralded careers. Many of those world-renowned players came to Spartan Stadium to play against the San Jose Earthquakes.

In February 1975, due to the shattering success of the Quakes' inaugural season and their league-leading home attendance figures the previous year, the NASL officially named San Jose "Soccer's First Super City." As a result of that declaration, the league awarded San Jose both the championship game of a new indoor league, taking place in March, as well as the main NASL championship game, to be held that August.

Beginning that year, in attempts to further Americanize the vernacular and mimic the Super Bowl format, the NASL began to call its championship game the Soccer Bowl. And beginning that year, the championship took place in a predetermined stadium, just like the Super Bowl. San Jose was awarded the first one.

But on the East Coast, Pelé's 1975 arrival in the United States that summer to play for the New York Cosmos changed everything. When he eventually came to Spartan Stadium, he changed everything in San Jose as well. The 1975 Soccer Bowl took place in San Jose on August 24, and Pelé came with the Cosmos to play an exhibition game three days later. The Brazilian superstar arrived in San Jose for all of the festivities surrounding both events.

The 1975 Soccer Bowl proved to be a star-studded affair. Future Olympic decathlon gold medalist and San Jose State graduate Bruce Jenner kicked out the first ball. Lou Rawls sang the national anthem. The attendance of 17,483 filled the stadium. Both teams in the championship, the Portland Timbers and the Tampa Bay Rowdies, were expansion franchises composed almost entirely of British players. Not one single American started for either side in the match.

Chris Dangerfield, who eventually emerged as a star for the Quakes in later seasons, started for that Portland squad. Recalling the preliminary events at the old San Jose Hyatt House on North First Street leading up to the Soccer Bowl, Dangerfield said Pelé was the consummate gentleman, accessible to everyone. "I remember the lads sitting at a poolside table and just chilling out, and Pelé came in with his entourage and personally came over and spent maybe twenty, thirty minutes just talking to us about the upcoming game and congratulating us and just basically wanted to know a little bit more about us," said Dangerfield. "This is Pelé for God's sakes, and that's what was different about the NASL. You had all these superstars, but in their own right, they were all just normal guys. They were great, and you could really just get close to them and they would spend a lot of their free time just getting to know you better."

Three days after the 1975 Soccer Bowl at Spartan Stadium, the Quakes defeated Pelé and the Cosmos 3–2 in front of 19,338 people, a few thousand over the stadium's capacity. People sat on the dirt hill behind the north goal and even hung from the trees to get a glimpse of the sport's all-time greatest player.

Many of the NASL-era Earthquakes players who battled against Pelé place him in context of the league in general. Before Paul Child came to the United States, for example, he was stuck in the reserves at Aston Villa, where club honchos told him he'd go no further. Laurie Calloway, likewise from Birmingham, played hundreds of games for third- and fourth-division English clubs. In the cases of both players, they would never have squared off against Pelé had they stayed in England. They would never have played in the same league as Cruyff, Beckenbauer or Eusebio.

"In a way, all of us on the San Jose Earthquakes team grew up watching a lot of these guys, never really getting an opportunity to ever play against them before," Child said. "Here we are at Spartan Stadium, a place with

Above: Pelé, Lou Rawls and Bruce Jenner with the San Jose Earthquakes Shakers at the 1975 NASL championship game (Soccer Bowl 1975), Spartan Stadium. *Debbie Hilpert.*

Right: Soccer Bowl 1975 tickets (NASL Championship game, 1975). *History San Jose.*

twenty-two thousand people, and people hanging in the trees trying to get a seat to watch the game. I always seem to remember, too, that we always used to let off a bunch of fireworks, and the fog used to stay over the top of the field. It just made it more surreal. When you walked down the ramp, you saw all these people and you knew you were going to get on the field and play with Beckenbauer, Pelé and Neeskens and every great player in the world."

San Jose defeated the Cosmos and Pelé a year later also. In August 1976, the legends came back to town during the regular season, and the Quakes prevailed again, this time by a margin of 2–1, in front of 23,048 fans at Spartan Stadium. At the time, it was the largest attendance for any sporting event in San Jose history. The team installed extra grandstands just for Pelé's appearance. "They actually put seats in front of the wall," Kemp said. "If you can visualize it, at Spartan Stadium, the wall by the sidelines…they had seats in front of it. So when I'm taking a throw-in, I turn around and I'm literally sitting on your lap. They were also sitting in the trees behind the end-zone benches."

Pelé enters the field at Spartan Stadium to play with the New York Cosmos against the San Jose Earthquakes, August 27, 1975. *Debbie Hilpert.*

In the late 1970s, even after Pelé had retired but when the Cosmos were still champions, Child says the Quakes wanted to know they could compete with those kinds of players at their level. That's why defeating Pelé twice was such a fantastic memory. "I think that's what was so great about the games we played against the New York Cosmos," Child recalled. "We really had our opportunity at getting to play against probably one of the best teams in the world at the time. Beating them was the biggest thrill because who would have ever expected that?"

Field Manager Brian Holmes, originally from England, recalls Pelé with the utmost respect. Echoing Dangerfield's assessment, he says Pelé had no ego whatsoever. He was a consummate gentleman. "It didn't matter who you were or your race, color, creed—whatever you want to call it. He'd talk to everybody he could talk to," said Holmes. "He wasn't afraid to shake hands and talk. It doesn't matter if you were the lowest person on the totem pole or top dog. He just talked to everybody. And he was a nice, classy act."

The Quakes were not without their own slew of foreign-born superstars. Benfica legend Tony Simoes was already a national hero and a godlike figure in his home country of Portugal, having played in the 1966 World Cup. He eventually came to San Jose for the 1976 and 1977 seasons. When people talk about the NASL, the names usually mentioned include Pelé, Beckenbauer, Johann Cruyff, Eusebio, Carlos Alberto, Gerd Mueller and others. But hardly anyone talks about Tony Simoes, who was at least as good as the rest of them. "Everybody absolutely loved him," Kemp recalled. "He had great vision, was skilled [and had] just a slight frame, like the George Best build. But vision, control, touch…he was just a great player."

On the Slavic front, Quakes player and coach Gabbo Gavric, who'd previously played for the Oakland Clippers teams, became the very heart and soul of the San Jose Earthquakes. He operated and coached with a fighting spirit, an intense working-class ethic and a never-say-injured approach to the game. Unless something was actually broken, then you weren't injured. "Gabbo was a hard player," Kemp said. "[As a coach], he was down to earth, very straightforward. If you gave him 100 percent, he'd support you to the end. He didn't appreciate egos…he didn't appreciate people who didn't try. He asked for the best in a player and supported you to the end." Moore agreed: "In his presence, the way he made you feel, you never wanted to give anything less than 100 percent. That was Gabbo." (On a side note, Gavric had also spent the 1969 season as a placekicker for the San Francisco 49ers. At the time, he was one of the oldest rookies in the history of the NFL.)

San Jose's Gabbo Gavric taking on the New York Cosmos, 1975. *History San Jose.*

Even when the Quakes stumbled through two straight 8-22 seasons, in 1978 and 1979, the guerrilla marketing and promotional operation continued. Even after Mandaric had sold the team so he could then buy the Connecticut Bicentennials and move them to Oakland, where they became the Stompers, fans in San Jose continued to connect with the Earthquakes on a street level. The Oakland team lasted only one year before moving to Edmonton, so Mandaric eventually returned as the Quakes' owner in 1980, just as San Jose State University began to increase its connection with the professional squad.

EASY LIKE LAW SCHOOL

Easy Perez, a Sunnyvale High School graduate, was part of a crew of San Jose State University Spartans drafted by the Earthquakes during the years 1979–80, a crew that also included Steve "Red" Ryan and Derek Evans. Even before the NASL folded in 1985, Perez was already applying to law school and planning his next career, a legal practice that still exists today.

Currently, Perez's law office sits on the fifth floor of the SunWize Technology Building in downtown San Jose. A circa 1981 photo of Perez and fellow Quake George Best adorns the wall opposite his desk. Occupying essentially the entire north side of St. John Street, between Market and San

George Best promo shot, 1980. *History San Jose.*

Pedro, the twelve-story building overlooks the San Pedro Square Public Market, a relatively new urban development project spearheaded by former San Jose mayor Tom McEnery and his partners.

As we sat there in his office in 2014, Perez tossed his cellphone onto his desk and played a voice message from a long-lost fan in Arizona who'd grown up with the Quakes. The fan hadn't heard Perez's name in decades and was just now making contact, thanks to a mutual friend. The enthusiastic fan was carrying on for several minutes into Perez's voicemail about how much those teams meant to him, thanking Perez for supplying his family with tickets to every game and saying how Perez had been his idol thirty-four years ago.

As we talked, Perez elaborated on the Quakes' grand scheme of guerrilla marketing that still blanketed San Jose streets in the late '70s and early '80s, thanks to what Dick Berg originally started. Berg had long since moved on to other pursuits, but his promotional strategies remained. As a result, Perez appeared at grade schools all across Santa Clara County. "We did a ton of clinics at schools," he told me. "We'd go out to all the schools in the valley here, and they received us with open arms. When we did assemblies, we'd get there with two or three players...sometimes a Shaker would come with us. We'd get everybody in the gym, and we'd show them how to juggle, how to keep the ball up, how to pass, how to shoot."

Then came the marketing. Tickets always flowed.

"For someone who could juggle ten times, we'd give them tickets," Perez said. "That was our marketing strategy. Give tickets to the youth because they obviously have to come with their parents. And everybody likes it—the kids like it, their parents like it and it grows."

Throughout the NASL era, youth soccer for boys and girls exploded all over San Jose and Santa Clara County, thanks to the San Jose Earthquakes. The aftershocks can still be felt today. Basically, the reason why everyone's kids play soccer now is because of what these characters helped accelerate in the 1970s.

"Every youth soccer team would call the Earthquakes office and say, 'Can we get an Earthquake player at one of our practices?'" Perez said. "We were all over the place."

As we sat there in his law office, I got the feeling that no one usually asked Perez about any of this. He leaned back, hands behind his head, and glowed with authentic gratitude that he got a chance to play alongside George Best, one of the most natural geniuses to have ever graced the pitch.

Simply the Best

George Best was the first-ever rockstar footballer, essentially inventing the concept. Originally from Belfast, Northern Ireland, he rose to fame as a teenager, playing for Manchester United during the swinging '60s. Since his ascent to stardom paralleled the rise of the Beatles, fans dubbed him the Fifth Beatle or, in the Spanish-speaking countries, *El Beatle*. Compared to the current day, when players generally specialize in one or two components of the game—speed, possession, dribbling, set pieces, holding capability, prowess in the air, poaching in front of the net, etc.—Best excelled at all of the above. He was a naturally gifted player who could do just about anything on the pitch. For him, it wasn't even work. In particular, Best never took dives. Defenders constantly tried to kick the daylights out of him, yet he would never go down. If he did go down, though, he'd get right back up and somehow miraculously collect the ball anyway, leaving the defender standing, scratching his head and wondering what had just happened.

He drove fast cars, women fell at his feet and people wrote songs about him. Even though he never played in a World Cup, to this day, legions continue to argue that he was the greatest of all time. As his ex-wife, Angie,

George Best answering questions from reporters, 1980. *Dave Obenour.*

called to our attention in her 2001 book, *George and Me*: "George was not only the first superstar player, he was the first to throw mud at the referee, the first to wear his shirt out of his shorts, the first to get sent off a number of times, the first not to show up at a game. The superstar players today get quite a bit more leeway in the game because of the things George did three decades earlier."

In other words, the entire stage David Beckham walks on as a pop star was built by George Best. The reason Christiano Ronaldo employs bodyguards now, in 2015, is because of what George Best started.

By the time Best made it to San Jose, where he and Angie lived near Courtside in Los Gatos, and during the time in which their son Calum was born at Good Samaritan Hospital, Best was past his prime, but he still showed flashes of incomparable genius. Unfortunately, his lifelong battles with alcoholism had finally caught up with him, and he began to miss many games, instead opting for bars and pubs around town when he was supposed to be on the field.

Regardless of Best's ups and downs, his scoring career came to a poignant denouement forty-five miles south of San Francisco. And it was in San Jose that he scored what many consider to be his most sublime masterpiece of a goal.

On July, 22, 1981, out of defiant individualism, contrarian grandiosity and perhaps even sheer genius, Best scored a goal against the Fort Lauderdale Strikers that people in San Jose and throughout the world still talk and write about thirty-four years later.

Beginning with a free kick, Best played the ball to a teammate, who then played it right back to him. From there, in shimmy, borderline-surfing fashion, Best proceeded to dribble twenty yards past half of the Fort Lauderdale team and straight into the six-yard box before slotting a shot past keeper Jan van Beveren. In the process, opposing players seemed to collapse left and right, a few times without Best even touching the ball. None of them could tell which direction Best was going at any given fraction of a second. Ironically, Ray Hudson and Thomas Rongen, both of whom went on to coach several MLS teams, were among those Best outmaneuvered on the play.

That evening, there were 11,629 of us in the stands. Almost every person, young or old, will say that goal was the best one he or she has ever seen. In Best's autobiography, *Blessed*, he wrote that it was the best one he ever scored, and many claim it was the best goal in the entire seventeen-year history of the North American Soccer League. One YouTube video of the tally boasts over 2.3 million views. When Best's name comes up in any conversation in San Jose, that goal is usually the first thing people mention, whether they were at the game or not. For those of us who were, no one had seen anything like it.

Best lasted the rest of the 1981 campaign and then played only a handful of games during the 1981–82 indoor season. His battles with alcoholism continued to escalate, and the team finally cut him loose as the 1982 outdoor preseason was just starting. After that famous goal against Fort Lauderdale in July 1981, Best scored just three more times during the 1981 season for a total of thirteen tallies. That made it twenty-one total that he netted for San Jose in his two years, with an additional thirty-two goals during two indoor seasons, 1980–81 and 1981–82. After a career that put him on top of the world as a teenager, right as the swinging '60s were unfolding, Best scored his final professional goals while playing for the San Jose Earthquakes.

The Quakes of 1982 were in dismal shape, not just on the field but in the bank as well. As the 1982 NASL season commenced, the league had once again imploded, this time dropping from twenty-one teams to fourteen. As the buzzards began to circle the league, and with rumors of the Quakes going

The Earthquakes' Johnny Moore and Pelé at Spartan Stadium, 1975. *History San Jose.*

broke and/or relocating, the Mandaric ownership group began to search for a new cadre of people who could at least keep the team in San Jose.

Johnny Moore, then back with the team as assistant general manager, brokered a meeting with Michael D'Addio, whose company, Corvus Systems, was headquartered near the Earthquakes' offices. D'Addio then went to his friend real estate developer Carl Berg, and the two of them assembled a "syndicate"—to use D'Addio's word—in order to take over the franchise. It was Moore who can be credited for initially bringing D'Addio's group into the fold, all to help keep the team in San Jose. "It was way more than a job to Johnny," D'Addio told me. "It was a love affair with the team and the city. And he did his best."

WHERE IS GOLDEN BAY?

After the 1982 outdoor season, the league was clearly battling financial troubles, and teams began to formulate additional indoor-league versions of themselves. Since no venue existed in San Jose in which to play indoor soccer, the team chose to play its indoor games in the Oakland Coliseum Arena. At this juncture, under the syndicate of Berg, D'Addio and GM John Carbray, the San Jose Earthquakes renamed themselves the Golden Bay Earthquakes in order to dangle some carrots at the indoor fans in Oakland. Since the San Francisco Bay has not ever been referred to as Golden Bay, as there exists no such place, the decision was widely panned.

In the *San Jose Mercury-News*, Fred Guzman famously asked, "Where is Golden Bay?" No one seemed to know.

For many native San Jose fans, the decision was a belligerent slap in the face. After Dick Berg and Milan Mandaric had famously fought the league for a San Jose–based team years earlier, after their hard work had led to San Jose's first-ever major professional sports team, the whole geographical moniker issue, and with it the inferiority complex, had come full circle. Even with a new upper deck at Spartan Stadium increasing its capacity by ten thousand, it now seemed like the team was embarrassed to name itself after San Jose. Dionne Warwick would have been proud.

In any event, the outdoor team still played its games at Spartan Stadium, and the 1983 season proved to be the best one to date. Berg and D'Addio can be credited for putting money toward reviving a dying squad. New coach Don Popovic eventually helped assemble a world-class selection of players, and the Quakes' efforts led to a stellar season in which they went undefeated at home. It was an all-star side with players like Steve Zungul from Yugoslavia; Godfrey Ingram and Chris Dangerfield, both originally from the UK; Leonardo Cuellar from Mexico; Fernando Clavijo from Uruguay; Stan Terlecki from Poland; and Americans like Mike Hunter.

Dangerfield, like many before him in the NASL, was another example of a European player who went on to make San Jose his permanent home. To this day, he still claims that the 1983 squad was one of the best teams the Quakes ever fielded, in any era. "We were just a wonderfully talented attacking team," Dangerfield said. "Don Popovic…his training sessions may have not been the most tactically astute, but he certainly knew how to pick a player. He had a great eye for talented players and how to mash them into a working unit. I think from those days of playing indoor soccer and being a success over at the New York Arrows, where he coached for many years, he just loved flair players who are very good at attacking, and our team was made up of those."

All did not end well, however. The team's record-setting season came to a shattering conclusion as Toronto ultimately squashed San Jose in the semifinals. It was a heartbreaking loss, especially after Berg and D'Addio

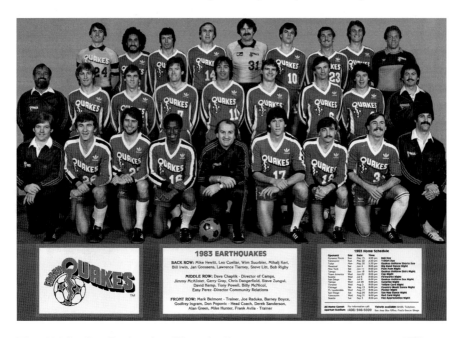

The 1983 San Jose Earthquakes. *History San Jose.*

had gone out of their way, heroically rescuing a floundering franchise and hiring Popovic, who became the 1983 NASL Coach of the Year.

Following the 1983 season, the buzzards continued to circle the league from above. More teams began to fold, and when the 1984 season started, only nine teams were left. Peter Bridgwater, former GM of the Vancouver Whitecaps during that team's 1979 championship season, took over as the Quakes' general manager and would eventually go on to become one of the most important purveyors of the game in the entire Bay Area for years to come. But the writing was on the wall for the NASL. Even with fielding additional indoor teams to make a profit, many squads could no longer survive financially. No one from the beginning had ever devised a logical business plan for the long term, and attendance figures were plummeting. Especially following owner Steve Ross's departure from the Cosmos, every last ounce of inspirational fuel in the league tank was empty.

The final Earthquakes match in the NASL, a road game against the New York Cosmos, took place on September 12, 1984, with the Quakes winning 1–0 on a Godfrey Ingram goal. The attendance of 7,581 was the lowest ever for a Cosmos match at Giants Stadium. Despite the win, and despite San Jose's Steve Zungul and Branco Segota leading the depleted league in scoring, the Quakes finished dead last in the standings.

At the end of the season, convinced the league was essentially kaput and wouldn't be around the following year, Berg decided he could not lose any more money. He incrementally sold off the players and ended the Golden Bay Earthquakes.

Berg, who would go on to carve out a billion-dollar-plus real estate portfolio in Silicon Valley, would later talk about the Quakes' days in Rotary Club speeches: "I lost $8 million, but it was the funnest time I ever had."

Back east, plans still existed for a 1985 outdoor season, but by then, only two teams were left to participate: Toronto and Minnesota. Even the mighty New York Cosmos, now under the control of Giorgio Chinaglia, could not post a bond guaranteeing they'd be able to complete the season. With that, no other course of action was possible, so the NASL suspended operations on March 28, 1985.

Lifelong Earthquakes fan Tony Huston grew up in the NASL era and recalls sitting there in the stands as a teenager during the league's final days. At one particular game (he can't remember exactly which one), GM Peter Bridgwater came onto the field at halftime to confirm what many had suspected: the NASL was just about kaput. "I was just devastated," Huston recalled. "On one hand, it was cool because he was open and honest, saying,

'This is it. The league's folding, but we're going to do everything we can to keep things going here and create a new league.' But it was devastating to me because the Quakes were my entire life...I wanted to leave—I didn't want to be there anymore. It was like everything was over."

Huston even recalled that the theme from *Chariots of Fire* was playing when Bridgwater made the announcement. Huston characterized the tune as "shitty-ass sad music." "Music obviously has a huge impact," Huston said. "It sets the mood for so many things, so it's easy for me to remember."

Countless others who grew up with the Quakes have similar stories of heartbreak when the league folded. Many of that generation simultaneously grew up watching programs like *Soccer Made in Germany* on public television or were children of immigrants and were schooled on the game as the Quakes evolved. San Jose fans were knowledgeable, familiar with the foreign leagues and the World Cup teams. They knew soccer was the world's game, the universal language and also the first pro sport San Jose could call its own.

Throughout parts of the rest of the world—Europe in particular—people are born with the neighborhood football club flowing through their bloodstream. Historically speaking, in certain towns with absolutely nothing else to do, the club became everything to the people who grew up there, primarily because the club was all the town had. This was somewhat akin to San Jose in the 1970s. Fans were just plain frustrated when the team ceased to exist in 1984.

But when recalling the NASL era years later in 2009, Guzman suggested the Quakes just might have captured lightning in a bottle. With perfect timing in San Jose's history, they sowed the seeds to help grow a game while putting San Jose on a pro sports map for the very first time. "What they did...it may have been a very important step into making San Jose more than a little jerkwater town in the minds of people," said Guzman. "Because all of a sudden—and there's a lot to be said of this—when you look at the standings, you're in standings with places like New York. That wasn't happening in anything else. You're in the standings with all the other big cities in the country. You weren't playing Fresno State."

Obenour agreed: "The Earthquakes were the first truly professional franchise in this town. People talk about the old college football programs, but the Quakes were the first big-time sports franchise."

In particular, it can be understood that the first two San Jose Earthquakes seasons—when they led the league in attendance—and how the team first took to the streets en masse and brought the game to the general public, before the Cosmos' notoriety had exploded, were precisely what gave

Trainer Dave "Obie" Obenour (in shorts) looks on from the sideline, 1976. *Dave Obenour.*

the NASL a new optimism and also what essentially launched the sport's popularity in the United States.

"They can probably count on, historically, being the group that probably built soccer in America," Dick Berg told me. "It was a small town, San Jose. This wasn't Los Angeles, New York City or even Dallas. When you suddenly said 'San Jose' all around the country, it was like, 'Gee, how did they do it?' And out of that—it took years—but I think it's what built soccer. San Jose was always a symbol of success. People thought, 'If they can do it, we can do it.'"

As the sixty-six-year-old Johnny Moore and I commandeered a table at the Britannia Arms Pub in downtown San Jose on a warm summer evening during the 2014 World Cup, a giant "USA Soccer 2014" banner hung from the rafters across the patio. Surrounding the patio, myriad televisions broadcasted highlights of the games earlier in the day.

"Our goal was to grow the game," Moore said, motioning with his head toward the highlight reels on the TVs. "Has the game grown? Yes. Just look at ESPN's ratings in this World Cup. Has the game grown? Yes, beyond our belief. Beyond our belief. So yes, the NASL was unbelievably successful. The North American Soccer League had a huge role in the growth of the

San Jose Earthquakes training session, 1975. *History San Jose.*

game in this country. I believe it was the most significant piece of the puzzle, without any question."

In another conversation, Guzman had already concurred. Just like in other parts of the country, NASL players, including many originally from Europe, eventually made permanent homes in their respective cities, where they continued to lobby for the sport decades later.

"The NASL…spread seeds all over the country," Guzman said. "All those guys—there's so many of those guys who played with the Quakes—who were 'foreigners' never left. And they spread the seeds, coaching, doing clinics—they continued to spread the gospel years later. The same thing happened in Seattle and Portland and in many, many other places, especially places that didn't have a large immigrant community."

CHAPTER 6

TRANSITION STATE

The passage of time between the death of the NASL in 1985 and the reincarnation of the San Jose Earthquakes in Major League Soccer (MLS) can be understood as a Buddhist-style bardo state of transition. At first, the times were dark, indeed, but from the ashes of the NASL through the rest of the 1980s and into the early 1990s, the sport eventually began to rise again. From a loose-knit conglomeration of amateur and semipro talent, various schemes emerged.

In 1985, after acquiring the rights from Berg and D'Addio to use the team's logo and colors, Peter Bridgwater changed the name back to the San Jose Earthquakes and tried to keep the game afloat by co-founding the Western Alliance Challenge Series, which included three other indie squads: FC Portland, FC Seattle and the Victoria Riptide from British Columbia. All four teams essentially straddled the gray area between amateur and semipro, with an assemblage of former NASL players, local university talent and other interested parties. At first, each team played seven games, including a few against the Edmonton Brickmen and Canada's national side. NASL Quake Laurie Calloway coached San Jose. At the end of the series, the Earthquakes took first place and defeated Victoria in the championship match at Spartan Stadium. In the 2–1 victory, Chris Dangerfield scored the winning goal with less than five minutes to play.

With a predominantly American team, the Quakes' vision was to eventually build a new league, including a development league, in order for the system to grow. The whole endeavor proved to be fruitful enough to officially spawn the Western Soccer Alliance, which began in 1986. That year, three other teams entered the fray: the San Diego Nomads, the LA Heat and the Seattle Storm.

For San Jose, Brian Holmes reprised his role as field manager and printer of uniform, and he also maintained a financial interest in the squad and functioned as de facto assistant manager. He explained the reason for Bridgwater's insistence on an "alliance."

"If you're called an alliance, you're not a league," Holmes told me. "If you're a league, you have to pay dues to U.S. Soccer. And [Bridgwater] didn't want to have to pay dues."

The "alliance" was barely even a semipro endeavor. Everyone had other jobs, and the players trained a few times a week. When playing away matches, this new version of the Quakes would not even get hotel rooms. For example, they'd fly down to San Diego, ride in vans, eat at McDonald's and then eventually warm up, play the match and fly right back afterward. Holmes often drove them around. "If they started the game, they got paid seventy-five bucks," Holmes said. "If they came off the bench, they got fifty bucks."

With virtually no budget, the team "office" on Stevens Creek Boulevard consisted of only a few people, including Fred Guzman, who was now the PR director. Tony Huston, still a teenager, often showed up to help out. Bridgwater gave him promotional materials to distribute, plus other odds and ends. "They handed us all these calendar schedules, and we had to go put 'em up in liquor stores," Huston recalled. "On quite a few days, I took the County Transit bus to the office, with my bike, and got all these calendars. They'd tell me where to go, and I'd take the bus out there and ride around to all these liquor stores and put posters up."

On game days, the teenage helpers would arrive four hours before the match in order to help out on the field, in the locker rooms and in the press box, where maybe three reporters would occupy the whole box. Huston worked as a volunteer gopher of sorts. The team had so few resources to work with that even the teenagers got railroaded into doing whatever they could to pull off the logistics.

"For one game," said Huston, "I can't remember what team it was that we played, but they had come into town, they had beaten the Quakes and they wanted to go party, but there was nobody available to drive the bus. I was only fourteen and a half or fifteen at the time, never driven in my life. And next thing I know, I'm actually driving this team to the Britannia Arms on Almaden Expressway."

The San Jose Earthquakes of the 1987 Western Soccer Alliance. *History San Jose.*

Bridgwater had many international connections, so to help finance his new transitional semipro San Jose Earthquakes, he organized numerous high-profile international matches at Spartan Stadium for capacity crowds. In 1985, Diego Maradona, then playing for Napoli in Italy, arrived for an exhibition match against UNAM Pumas of Mexico. The Argentine superstar and his grandiose demands proceeded to wreak havoc on the organizers. One of San Jose's popular hotels in those days was the Red Lion Inn by the airport, now reflagged as the Doubletree. It was not good enough for Maradona. "He didn't like the sheets," Holmes recalled, "because they were white and they were cotton sheets. He told Peter [Bridgwater] they have to be black and they have to be satin. So Peter says, 'Brian, go find him some black satin sheets.' And I said, 'You gotta be kidding me.' So I go into the lobby, and I get on the phone. I get out the phone book, and I start calling around. Nobody's got 'em in San Jose. I end up driving to San Francisco to get sheets for his bed."

Bridgwater's international matches throughout the 1980s proved to be successful (Manchester City at Spartan Stadium for eight dollars!), but when all was said and done, the era had not fostered mass local optimism for the game. For fans and players, the era was one of post-league heartbreak and longing—a dark, dismal era characterized by vanishing talent, revenue and fan support. After the dizzying implosion of the NASL, major investors had no interest in going at it one more time, and the semipro nature of the team simply didn't cut it. There was no Pelé, George Best, Tony Simoes or

Gabbo Gavric; no mass outreach to the fans on the streets; and no budget. Players carried on for the sheer love of the game, and that was it. The San Jose Earthquakes of the Western Soccer Alliance never drew more than two thousand fans during their short existence.

Nevertheless, there was always hope for another resurgence of professional soccer in San Jose. Bridgwater and Holmes were still optimistic. "I always thought that one day, another league would come out of this," Holmes recalled. "I thought this league would just keep growing. I don't know what other people were thinking, but I know Peter's dream was for it to expand."

But after a few more seasons of trying to make something work, Bridgwater sold the team to Bill Lunghi and a few other partners before the 1988 season, staying on as GM. The new ownership group could not accomplish anything financially, and after one year of their stewardship, the team pulled out of the league and ultimately went under. By then, the Western Soccer Alliance had morphed into the Western Soccer League, and after the demise of the Earthquakes, the league had awarded a new team to Dan Van Voorhis, a Bay Area real estate attorney. Naming the squad the San Francisco Bay Blackhawks after one of his own housing development projects, Van Voorhis launched his new team in the 1989 season.

From there, thanks to Van Voorhis, a new, more heavily financed era of local soccer began to emerge, and things began to reinvent themselves once again. At first, the team played its home games at different venues all over the Bay Area. Recalling those days, Dominic Kinnear, who played midfield for the team, said he approved of the concept. One game, they'd play at Pioneer High School in San Jose, the next, in San Ramon. One match would unfold at Monta Vista High School in Cupertino and the next one in Saratoga. "Dan [Van Voorhis] tried to reach every facet of soccer fans of the area," Kinnear said. "It may look kind of crazy, but when you think about it, it was a pretty good idea. Rather than have people come to the game, the game was kind of coming to you."

However, just as the Blackhawks were getting started by playing games at various spots throughout the Bay Area and building what became one of the best teams in the United States, more of the old San Jose Earthquakes players from previous incarnations still lurked beneath the surface. In one case, Quakes alumni from the 1970s threw together a full-blown reunion against the 1975 Portland Timbers squad. Since Chris Dangerfield had played for both those teams, he played one half for each squad in the reunion match, just like Pelé had done in his retirement match between the Cosmos and Santos of Brazil.

The 1989 reunion match, Spartan Stadium. George Best at left. *Frankie Smillie.*

Eventually, the WSL merged with its East Coast equivalent, the American Soccer League, to form the American Professional Soccer League (APSL), in which the San Francisco Bay Blackhawks participated for the next three seasons.

In the early 1990s, when barely anything more than ill repute still populated Santa Clara Street in downtown San Jose, the Blackhawks' team office was located at Second and Santa Clara, in a spot now occupied by a craft beer establishment. One could saunter down the grimy thoroughfare, stare right into the window and see flags from storied international teams the Blackhawks had played exhibition matches against, clubs like Kaiserslautern, Benfica or Mexico City's Club America. It was like an exotic oasis amid the surrounding drugs, prostitution and homelessness of that street. There still seemed to be hope for the world's game to flourish in San Jose.

And in time, hope did emerge, as the Blackhawks became one of the better squads in American soccer during those years, including several players who capped for the U.S. National Team. Several went on to play in the 1994 World Cup and/or went on to star in Major League Soccer.

In particular, the 1991 team won the national championship, defeating the Albany Capitals in the finals. By then, most Blackhawks regular-season home games were taking place at Newark Memorial Stadium, but the playoff matches took place at Spartan, including the final of the away-and-home championship series against Albany, which went to penalties.

Original San Jose Earthquakes defender Laurie Calloway coached that 1991 side, which featured a lineup that read like an all-star team of Americans who played the game at that time. Blackhawks like Eric Wynalda and Marcelo Balboa put in numerous appearances for the U.S. National Team, and Jeff Baicher, Paul Bravo and Troy Dayak eventually went on to star for San Jose when Major League Soccer first began play in 1996.

In another instance, and one of tag-team duplicity that brought everything full circle, Blackhawks midfielder Dominic Kinnear went on to not only play for San Jose in MLS but also assistant-coach the team during its 2001 and 2003 MLS Championships and then coach the team to a 2005 Supporters' Shield trophy, given to the squad with the best record in the league. Blackhawks defender John Doyle eventually went on to become the first officially signed San Jose player when MLS started, as well as the team's first captain. When Kinnear became San Jose's coach in 2004–05, Doyle became his assistant coach. The two were childhood friends who grew up attending Earthquakes matches at Spartan Stadium during the 1970s. And both were Blackhawks teammates.

At the time, Van Voorhis might have harbored grand schemes to help reestablish soccer in the Bay Area, but to Kinnear and many of the players, it was all about the game. Everyone was just excited to play and get paid. "It was honestly about playing," Kinnear recalled. "I think we all wanted to play. [We were] Bay Area guys. We had kind of been around the Earthquakes, but then that disappeared. So for this kind of team to start up...[we now had] a chance to play."

In Dayak's case, he was invited to become one of the founding members practically straight out of high school. After graduating in 1989, he was heading off to college, but the Blackhawks set up a trust fund to yank him from college and provide a subsequent multiple-year contract. It became clear that Van Voorhis was putting much more money into building a team and that a serious effort to make the squad professional was underway.

"It was starting off as a pro-amateur team but was going to turn into this big professional team on the West Coast," Dayak recalled. "I can remember having a conversation and sitting down with my parents about what that meant. But for me, as a teenager, you just want to play ball."

In the Blackhawks era, the local lineage seemed to resurface over and over again, in multiple layers, through all the ups and downs, with Britannia Arms on Almaden Expressway continuing to function as the de

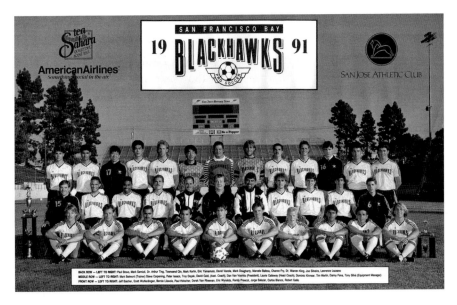

The 1991 San Francisco Bay Blackhawks, APSL champions. *History San Jose.*

facto street headquarters for many of the players. Bravo, the 1991 APSL Rookie of the Year, even wound up bartending at Britannia Arms during his stint with the Blackhawks.

But in the minds of many, the 1991 Blackhawks championship team is what still resonates deeply, as does the team's resulting run in the 1992 CONCACAF Champions Cup. In the former case, the team defeated the Albany Capitals in a thrilling comeback victory in front of 12,411 at Spartan Stadium. The latter scenario made history, as the Blackhawks became the first-ever professional team to represent the United States in a CONCACAF Champions tournament. The team reached the CONCACAF semifinals by winning five out of six preliminary matches before splitting a home-and-away series with Mexico's Club America and losing 4–3 on aggregate. In that series, Club America won the first game in Mexico City, and although the Blackhawks took the second match at Spartan Stadium on August 16, 1992, it was not enough to win the series. At the time, Club America was coached by none other than Hugo Sanchez, one of Mexico's all-time greatest players. The crowd of 24,200 at the second game set an all-time record for soccer matches at Spartan Stadium.

Kinnear simply remembers a great team of guys in their early twenties with great chemistry. They could run for days, and they just wanted to bring home a championship. "I look back, and I go, 'Talented team—a good group of individual soccer players,'" Kinnear said. "Let's be honest, Eric Wynalda was one of the best American soccer players of all time. It was right before he went to Germany and really did well over there. You had strength at every position, and it was a good group of guys. I think we seemed to enjoy each other's company…Just overall I thought we had a bright, talented team, and I thought we wanted to win. We were hungry. We didn't want to do anything except play soccer and try and win."

Dayak agreed: "I think there was a lot of motivation and drive in the players that were selected, and a lot of thought. There was a lot more to it than people realize; it was a lot more than just throwing a team together."

In short, the Blackhawks were arguably the strongest team in the United States at that time, even though the league was only a fraction of what the NASL once was. Even though I was an SJSU student and Spartan Stadium concessions stand worker at the time, that final Blackhawks squad (1991–92), in my opinion, would have fared quite strongly in the 1996 inaugural season of MLS, had the team remained intact until then.

Van Voorhis seemed to enjoy the camaraderie, buying the players fancy dinners on the road and simply providing owner support. He even personally delivered small bonuses to the players if they won high-profile matches. After the dismal semipro era of the Western Soccer League's San Jose Earthquakes, and stories of checks bouncing left and right, Van Voorhis investing money and giving players some extra dough seemed to prove he meant business.

"He would walk into the locker room and give everybody a small white envelope, and in that white envelope was a $100 bill," Kinnear recalled. "It didn't matter if you played the whole game or if you played five minutes or if you didn't play at all. He gave everybody the same. You have to remember, it was 1990–91, and we're getting paid. He was a great owner. When you got that $100 bill, you felt like you were rich."

Over the phone, Kinnear continued to emphasize that scenario. It felt special because, at the time, twenty-one- to twenty-two-year-old players weren't accustomed to making anything. "We all kind of came from humble beginnings, and there wasn't a lot of money getting thrown around," he said. "So you'd win a big game, and he would come in and give you a $100 bill in an envelope. And I ain't kidding you, you felt like you were king of the world. That's what kind of person he was—he made you feel that good."

Dayak, being the first-ever recipient of a five-year contract as a teenager—unheard of at the time—still cites Van Voorhis as a mentor. Dayak was likewise the recipient of several $100 handshakes. When Dayak

San Francisco Bay Blackhawks pennant. *History San Jose.*

played on the 1992 Olympic team in Barcelona or traveled with the U.S. Men's National Team, Van Voorhis would cover his flight if he needed to return back to the States and join the Blackhawks on the road somewhere.

To Dayak, Van Voorhis was a genuine person but volatile, with very high expectations. "At a young age, that's impressionable," Dayak told me. "It's something you remember because those are guiding factors in your life. He started my National Team career—he supported me in that."

Brian Holmes, who was then still reprising his role as field manager at Spartan Stadium, said the stories began to spread around the league. Other teams seemed to feel jealous. "It's amazing how many people wanted to play for the Blackhawks," Holmes recalled. "People were calling up all the time. When we played against other teams, the whole conversation would be, 'I can't believe how much they're paying you guys.' We were like the Cosmos of that little league because they were overpaid in comparison to the rest of the league. Other players were always asking if they could join the team."

As the Blackhawks were playing the best soccer in the country, winning a championship and holding their own against high-profile foreign teams, downtown San Jose was just beginning to reconstruct itself. A new light-rail system had debuted a few years earlier. Intermittent pieces of downtown's post–Dutch Hamann skid row landscape still lingered from the 1970s and 1980s, but a raging counterculture music scene, which included four particular clubs near the corner of First and San Salvador Streets, had emerged out of nowhere. Members of the Blackhawks occasionally showed up at the Ajax Lounge, an upstairs joint specializing in avant-jazz, roots and alternative sounds. I was also a regular, lurking in the shadows.

Especially in 1992, when Ipswich Town legend Paul Mariner arrived as a player/coach for the team under Laurie Calloway, the players would occasionally show up at Ajax. No one anywhere in the establishment seemed to have any idea that Mariner, the long-haired former star of the English National Team who was probably a household name in England and who'd won the UEFA Cup with Ipswich Town, was among their ranks. At that time, the English First Division was just beginning to rebrand itself into the Premier League, and I distinctly remember standing there at the Ajax Lounge after several cheap pints of beer, laughing at myself, wondering if I were the only one in the bar who even knew who Mariner was. Or Ipswich was. Or the Blackhawks were. Those were very alienating times to be a soccer enthusiast in San Jose, with the Blackhawks receiving next to no press coverage.

However, that would change. In July 1992, *Metro Silicon Valley*, the region's alternative weekly newspaper and the same publication that would eventually employ yours truly eleven years later, ran an exhaustive five-thousand-word cover story on Mariner and the Blackhawks. Staff writer Jonathan Vankin,

Jonathan Vankin's *Metro Silicon Valley* story on Paul Mariner of the San Francisco Bay Blackhawks.

who would later go on to write *The World's Greatest Conspiracies*, as well as edit Anthony Bourdain's graphic novel *Get Jiro!*, documented Mariner's entire career for several pages.

But after the 1992 season, the league inevitably began to stagnate. Just like the NASL, teams could not afford to keep up. Van Voorhis formally withdrew the team from the APSL, opting to compete in the lower-quality United States Interregional Soccer League (USISL) for the 1993 season before disbanding altogether in the wake of the upcoming 1994 World Cup. For their entire run, including all league games, playoffs, exhibitions and tournament contests, the Blackhawks' cumulative win/loss percentage was a staggering .713.

As preparations for the 1994 World Cup were underway in the United States, Peter Bridgwater was busy overseeing the San Francisco Bay Area venue Stanford Stadium. At the same time, preparations for a brand-new, full-blown league, eventually to be called Major League Soccer, were underway as well. Van Voorhis became the prime mover for San Jose's inclusion in that new league, which was initially scheduled to launch in 1995.

On San Jose's behalf, a committee of sports executives, politicians, newspapermen and local civic leaders all signed a fifty-page bid to include San Jose as one of the initial seed teams. Van Voorhis chaired the committee, which also included then–San Jose mayor Susan Hammer, then–San Francisco mayor Frank Jordan, U.S. senator Diane Feinstein, San Francisco Giants executive vice-president Laurence Bauer and San Jose State University president Handel Evans.

The bid proved to be successful, with Van Voorhis agreeing to sell what was left of the Blackhawks—assets, stocks and player contracts—to MLS. The initial deal, announced in December 1994, allowed MLS to acquire the Blackhawks team, including long-term rights to Spartan Stadium, with Van Voorhis becoming an MLS limited partner in exchange for the sale of his stock. In the end, it can be understood that Dan Van Voorhis and the Blackhawks are what directly led to San Jose becoming one of MLS's founding cities.

"We started a generation here on the West Coast where people could go watch pros play," Dayak said. "And really good pros…It really was the foothold of MLS. It gave a lot of people an opportunity to dream about something bigger, including the players and the fans…It really was the foundation for the MLS team—the Clash and the Earthquakes."

As MLS began to assemble itself, San Jose was chosen to host one of the founding franchises, along with Boston, Columbus, Los Angeles, New York/New Jersey and Washington, D.C. Other cities—Tampa Bay, Denver, Kansas City and Dallas—would come on board the following year, as the league decided to delay the beginning of play until 1996. The stage for MLS was now set.

Identity Clash

During the launching stages of MLS, the league collaborated with partners like Nike and Adidas to create tacky, single-syllable nicknames for the teams and place them in hideous, multicolored jerseys, which made everything seem as un-soccer-like as possible. It almost seemed like they were targeting 1990s emo kids at the mall rather than soccer fans. As a result, the San Jose soccer lineage began its MLS era nicknamed the Clash, and the team's logo was something resembling a scorpion. No one had any idea what it meant, but thankfully for the fans, it was less embarrassing than the Kansas City Wiz or the Dallas Burn. As the league began play, D.C. United was the only franchise out of the original ten that actually looked and sounded like an authentic football club, in the traditional sense. For example, Miami Fusion sounded more like a bad mall restaurant or a flavor of dinner jazz than a professional soccer club.

In any event, when MLS began, the league willfully distanced itself from the NASL era and its failings, but specific players, coaches and even owners carried on the lineage. Lamar Hunt, for example, still owner of the Kansas City Chiefs NFL team, and who had co-founded the NASL in the first place, also helped start Major League Soccer. When MLS launched, Hunt owned both the Kansas City and Columbus franchises, which helped give the league immediate credibility.

In San Jose's case, historical connections from years, or even decades, earlier emerged right off the bat. Peter Bridgwater became the president and general manager. Laurie Calloway became the coach and then signed John Doyle as the first official player, cementing a multigenerational lineage of San Jose history into the club from the very onset. Paul Bravo and Troy Dayak also came on board, adding to that lineage as the team's first draft pick and first trade, respectively. The league also allocated Eric Wynalda to San Jose, further establishing a Blackhawks reunion before the season even started.

When MLS officially began play, the inaugural game between D.C. United and San Jose took place on April 6, 1996, at Spartan Stadium. The home team stayed in the Fairmont Hotel in downtown San Jose before taking an inaugural bus ride to the stadium. Dayak remembers that bus ride as an incredible experience, seeing everyone outside on the street, walking to the game down Tenth Street and Seventh Street from downtown San Jose. "People were walking there with banners, flags [and] scarves—everyone just excited about MLS starting," Dayak told me. At the time, Dayak was still fairly young but had Olympic and National Team experience. To now see

The 1996 San Jose Clash. *John Todd/ISI Photos; San Jose Earthquakes.*

throngs of supporters back at Spartan Stadium to launch a new league was a powerful experience. "To see that in my hometown…it was just an incredibly proud moment to see fans that maybe we had started growing with the Blackhawks walking down the street, waving flags, jogging alongside the bus as we pulled in. Just the atmosphere was incredible—an awesome memory."

At the inaugural game, I was 1 of 31,683 in the stands that day. At that time, it was the largest crowd ever to attend a sporting event in San Jose. Eric Wynalda scored the winning goal for San Jose in the eighty-eighth minute, giving the Clash a 1–0 victory.

But before the game even started, Brian Holmes, once again reprising his role as field manager, saved the very first ball used in the match. It was a calculated, secret plan. "One of my jobs is to make sure there's ten brand-new balls to start the game," Holmes said. "That's an MLS rule—they want ten balls, all new. So I got the balls, went and pumped 'em all up and took them to the referee. And he says to me, 'Which one are we going to use to start the game?' And I said, 'Well, you pick the ball out, and I'll go from there.'"

After receiving what was to be the opening ball, Holmes took a felt pen and marked the ball so it could be identified after the match. He filled in the "o" in "soccer" underneath the MLS logo. Following the inaugural match, strict rules required the game balls go to various places—the San Jose front office, the U.S. Soccer Hall of Fame, MLS, the referee and one for D.C.

Eric Wynalda scores the first goal in MLS history. *John Todd/ISI Photos; San Jose Earthquakes.*

United, among others. As it turned out, only nine balls were allocated to go somewhere, so Peter Bridgwater told Holmes he could pick the one he wanted and take it for himself. "So I got the original ball that started the game," Holmes said. "Not the one that scored the goal, because they rotated around, but I got the one that started the game."

Just a few years ago, Holmes donated the ball to the Soccer Legacy Collection at History San Jose, a facility near Kelley Park, around the corner from Spartan Stadium, where it sits in storage along with hundreds of other mementos and ephemera from over forty years' worth of San Jose soccer history. To date, there exists no permanent venue in which to publicly exhibit all the items.

With Bridgwater and Calloway at the helm, the Clash finished its inaugural season with a 15-17 record, good enough to make the playoffs. Unfortunately, the Los Angeles Galaxy destroyed San Jose's hopes by knocking them out of the playoffs in the first round.

During the middle of the next season, Calloway was let go after escalating tensions between him and forward Eric Wynalda came to a head. Brian Quinn replaced him as coach but failed to take the team to the playoffs during any of his tenure, which lasted until the waning weeks of the 1999 season.

Change in the upper levels was already in the works before then, however. After three years of essentially functioning as a league-owned team, San Jose underwent a series of operational upheavals. Following the 1998 season, the Kraft Group, investor-operator of the New England Revolution MLS club and owner of the NFL's New England Patriots, took charge of the San Jose Clash. Lynne Meterparel became the new general manager.

While the team managed to win more games than it had in each of the previous three campaigns, Coach Quinn was sacked with only five games left in the 1999 season, making way for Lothar Osiander to replace him. Unfortunately, Osiander was unable to lift San Jose into the playoffs, and the squad finished the 1999 campaign with a 19-13 record, amounting to thirty-seven points.

But the drama did not stop there. After three straight years of failing to make the playoffs, what transpired during the offseason, in October 1999, proved to be a catalyst for many years to come. Changing the team's name back to the San Jose Earthquakes became a harbinger of fandom, new and old. It was a decision that incited emotions from a quarter century earlier and, from then on out, charted a new but uneasy path forward.

Sometimes the small decisions are the ones that go on to completely alter history in ways no one can predict. After spending much of the 1999 season

Troy Dayak on defense for the San Jose Clash. *John Todd/ISI Photos; San Jose Earthquakes.*

ratcheting up the outreach to season ticket holders via surveys, Meterparel made a conscious decision to rename the team the Earthquakes. She made the announcement on October 27 of that year, ridding forever the 1990s emo marketing schlock that Nike and MLS had inflicted on the entire franchise beginning in 1995. On that day, to unveil the return of the Quakes moniker, the team threw an official announcement press conference and party in front of the Fairmont Hotel and across the street in Plaza de Cesar Chavez. Brand-new MLS commissioner Don Garber attended the event. In Jodi Meacham's *San Jose Mercury-News* story the following day, Garber was quoted as saying, "This is a rebranding, which was driven by what the fans want. It's like an onion; we're peeling it all apart and then putting it back together in a way that works better for us."

No one knew what the implications, if any, of such a decision would be, and not everyone in the league supported Meterparel's decision. But the scenario, when viewed in historical retrospect, just might resemble what is known in chaos theory as the butterfly effect, or "sensitive dependency on initial conditions." Just as a butterfly waving its wings over Brazil might eventually trigger a series of events leading to a hurricane somewhere else in the world, the decision to reclaim San Jose's original pro sports moniker was exactly the initial condition needed to solidify the team's historical lineage years later. That one initial decision can be seen as the defining catalyst that oiled a brand-new machine of emotions.

Placing the moment in the lineage of the NASL and the Western Soccer Alliance years, some began to argue whether the team was Earthquakes 2.0 or 3.0, modeled after nomenclature used for software versions and updates. It made for good debate. As is often the case in the startup culture of Silicon Valley, failure is an acceptable and expected part of the process. Visionaries might start up a company, fail and then start another company, often more than once. Some serial entrepreneurs start several companies in their careers. It's a "build, break and start over" mindset. This is precisely what makes Silicon Valley different from the rest of the business world.

Former NASL Earthquakes Chris Dangerfield and Mark Demling did television commentary for the Clash when MLS first started. As Dangerfield and I spoke about it, he said the ridiculous decision to break with history by naming the team the Clash would eventually be relegated to a nonissue. It will be seen as a short, temporary era—not due to a lack of quality players (many went on to significant accomplishments) but because the Clash brand, which nobody understood, was just a dumb idea, first and foremost.

"I think it will be erased in some respects," Dangerfield told me. Many teams go through forgetting periods in their history, just as an English team might get relegated from the Premiership all the way down to the third division. "In the case of the Earthquakes," he said, "it wasn't so much going down to a lower league per se; it was just a change of name that did that. It would have been a lot easier, I think, if we'd have just kept it as the Earthquakes all the way through."

Dangerfield agreed with me that, had it been Bridgwater's decision, or that of anyone in San Jose, the team would have been called the Earthquakes from the start of MLS. After all, Bridgwater still claimed rights to the name and branding components. But it was out of his hands, thanks to league executives and a shoe company.

When the original moniker did return for the 2000 campaign, the effort proved futile on the field, as the Quakes went nowhere that year. They failed to make the playoffs again, finishing dead last in the entire league, with a 7-17-8 record. As a result, Meterparel resigned, and the Kraft Group exited from the operational front altogether. In the ashes of their departure, the San Jose Sharks NHL franchise stepped up to the plate as operators. A new era, with more solid local leadership, thus emerged.

CHAPTER 7

A NEW ERA

In what now seems like a complete overnight engine rebuild, the initial stages of what eventually unfolded as the league's first-ever bona fide worst-to-first turnaround began to take shape. In a rapid-fire series of hirings, personnel changes and draft picks, a new era emerged before anyone could understand that another era had just finished.

Silicon Valley Sports & Entertainment (SVS&E), the business arm of the Sharks, officially announced on January 10 that it was now the operator of the club. On that same day, MLS announced that Spartan Stadium would host the all-star game later that summer. Coach Osiander was promptly sacked, and Tom Neale came on board as general manager. Just a few weeks later, on February 2, Frank Yallop was named head coach.

Originally from England, Yallop grew up in Vancouver before hopping back across the pond to a career at Ipswich Town at age nineteen. After playing for Tampa Bay from 1996 to 1998, Yallop retired and became that team's assistant coach before landing the assistant coaching job at D.C. United for the 2000 season. At the time of Yallop's hiring in San Jose, he was thirty-six years old and had two working days to prepare for the MLS Superdraft, to be held on February 5. After putting together the beginnings of what was partly a brand-new squad, Yallop brought on former Bay Area Blackhawks and San Jose Clash player Dominic Kinnear as his assistant coach.

Then came the clincher. On March 29, the Quakes held a press conference at the Shark Tank, then known as the Compaq Center. At the event, General Manager Tom Neale announced the signing of Landon Donovan, who was

Frank Yallop and Landon Donovan at the podium when Donovan first signed with the San Jose Earthquakes, 2001. *John Todd/ISI Photos; San Jose Earthquakes.*

then nineteen years old and on loan from Bayer Leverkusen in Germany. Although I did not begin to cover the team until later that year, I attended that press conference, but in the capacity of someone from the general public. I never even knew if I was supposed to have access or not. I just heard about the event and wandered over, telling them I was a season ticket holder. It was just like sneaking down behind the goal at Spartan during the NASL games. No one seemed to care, so they let me in.

In the press release for that event, Yallop had this to say: "We think Landon will be a great addition to our team. He is a young player, but he has already shown with the National Team that he can compete at a high level. He is going to be one of the stars in U.S. soccer for many years."

Along with Donovan, other components brought into the fold by Neale, Yallop and Kinnear at that time helped form the core unit of what became one of the best teams in MLS from 2001 to 2005: Jeff Agoos, Dwayne De Rosario, Eddie Robinson, Ronnie Ekelund and a returning Troy Dayak, who'd previously been sidelined for over a year due to a near-paralyzing neck injury.

No one could have predicted the degree to which Donovan would become the poster boy for all of American soccer. The Quakes just knew they had a special young player in their ranks. Yallop had only watched Donovan in one previous match before he arrived in San Jose, as there wasn't nearly as much scouting video available back then as there is now. "I asked around, the people who had worked with him," explained Yallop. "They said fantastic things. I had no idea what I was getting, but after about twenty minutes to an hour of practice, it was like, 'Wow, we have a player.'"

The 2001 team emerged as a unique combination of veterans, young kids and those in between who still had something to prove. Everything started coming together during preseason.

Landon Donovan playing for the San Jose Earthquakes. *John Todd/ISI Photos; San Jose Earthquakes.*

"Frank was very smart, assessing which players should stay and which ones should go," said goalkeeper Joe Cannon, one of those who stayed. "All the dominoes just kind of fell into place. And then when we got Landon—and that was kind of later on in the preseason—he was a young kid, but you could tell right away he was good. But I don't think any of us imagined what he would turn out to be."

Yallop agreed: "Just watching him when he first came in…he was nineteen years old. He could run with the big boys, but he was still a kid. He changed his hairstyle five times in the time I was there. We had a laugh about that. It was orange, and it was blond and then black. He was doing all this young stuff, but what a player."

As what seemed like a brand-new Quakes team evolved, Landon likewise matured as a player, growing into the mix both as a teammate and a person. The rest of the squad, especially the veterans, realized Donovan's unique natural ability and helped mentor him in the process. After all, he was only a teenager.

Dayak, in particular, said it was amazing to watch Landon mature with the squad: "When we started practicing and training, Frank came to me and said, 'I'm putting this kid between you and Jeff Agoos, and you need to look after him and help him grow up and become a man in this sport.' Frank had an incredible understanding of what was needed to manage a team. I think we all knew that Landon was a special talent, a great individual talent and player, and it was our job to help him become a great team member, a team player."

Ever so humble, Yallop added: "I felt the team—and it's not the coaching—it was the team that developed him and made him feel welcome. They let him express himself within that team."

As the era progressed, Donovan blossomed into a natural superstar and would soon become the most recognizable American player the world's hugest sport had ever seen. As I began to cover the team for a now-defunct website, SlideTackleMagazine.com, and then later that year for *Metro Silicon Valley*, the region's alt-weekly newspaper, it felt like a true blessing to be a native San Jose journalist. There we were in a new era with the poster boy of U.S. soccer right here in town. In retrospect, just as I had been very lucky to see George Best at the end of his career when I attended matches as a little tyke, I was also very lucky to occupy the press box of the very same stadium and experience Landon Donovan beginning his career.

Five Earthquakes players went to the MLS all-star game that year, which just happened to be at Spartan Stadium. The match ended in a 6–6 draw

Landon Donovan playing for the San Jose Earthquakes, 2001. *John Todd/ISI Photos; San Jose Earthquakes.*

with Donovan getting four of the goals, including a hat trick in the first twenty minutes. He was named the game's MVP.

In the first round of the playoffs, San Jose walloped Columbus in two straight games, 3–1 and 3–0, before a dramatic semifinal showdown against the Miami Fusion. Coached by Ray Hudson—a former legend with Fort Lauderdale during the NASL days and also one of the players whom George Best had humiliated in his famous goal at Spartan Stadium exactly twenty years earlier—Miami came into the playoffs with the league's best record, but it was not good enough. The Quakes won the series in breathtaking fashion, with Dayak heading home the winning goal in overtime of the last game, at Miami, on Wednesday, October 17.

The MLS Cup, the championship match, was predetermined to take place at Columbus Crew Stadium, at that time the league's only soccer-specific facility. The match was just four days later, on the following Sunday.

"We didn't even come home," Cannon said. "We went straight from Miami to Columbus."

The match proved to be another nail-biter, with the Quakes giving up the first goal against the Los Angeles Galaxy before Donovan executed a world-class equalizer just before halftime. In overtime, Dwayne De Rosario, who'd entered the match earlier as a sub, scored the winning goal, bringing San Jose the championship.

"Frank was a very good coach back then," said Cannon. "He did an incredible job at really relating to players. If you weren't in the lineup, he would let you know why. He'd tell you what you're doing wrong and what you're doing right, but he connected. He tried to connect with everyone. And if you didn't make that connection with him, you probably weren't going to be there too long. He really went out of his way to try and cater to a player."

In 2002, the royal Quakes bloodline would get a new boost. Johnny Moore of the NASL era, the man who, along with Dick Berg, had launched the NASL club in the San Jose Hyatt House in 1974, came back into the fold as the team's general manager.

Also at the beginning of the season, SVS&E officially partnered with the Anshutz Entertainment Group (AEG) to become dual investor/operators of the team. Unfortunately, though, San Jose was unable to repeat as champion, even after winning twelve of fourteen home games that year. Columbus eventually got its revenge by knocking the Earthquakes out of the playoffs.

During the regular season, however, both Agoos and Donovan had successfully represented the Earthquakes with the U.S. Men's National Team at the 2002 World Cup in Japan and Korea, leading the United States to the quarterfinals for the first time ever. At age twenty, Donovan started each game, scoring two goals in the process. Although the Germans eventually

Landon Donovan playing for the San Jose Earthquakes, 2001. *John Todd/ISI Photos; San Jose Earthquakes.*

knocked the Americans out of the tournament on June 21, it was the United States' best World Cup to this day.

In an unprecedented maneuver, immediately following the U.S. team's exit from the World Cup, Donovan flew right back to San Jose, via Los

Angeles, and actually came onto the field for the Earthquakes the very next night against the Colorado Rapids. He came on as a sub less than forty-eight hours after he had walked off the pitch in Korea.

"He loved to play," recalled Cannon. "That's the thing about Landon. And when you're younger, that's the thing—you just want to play. Now, there's so many excuses for people: 'Oh, they just flew,' or 'You went across the country,' you know? But when we were younger, there was much less science involved. It was much more from the hip."

No soccer player in U.S. history has ever done such a thing, before or since. The Spartan Stadium crowd gave Donovan a standing ovation upon his entrance that evening.

Yallop added: "I think it shows the commitment to his team. I think that's Donovan. He wants to get back. He doesn't need time off. At that point, obviously, he's twenty years old and flying with his career. What a welcome he had."

Following the 2002 season, it was still unclear whether Donovan would stay in the United States or return to Bayer Leverkusen in Germany. When all was said and done, enough people convinced him to remain in California, and he signed another two-year loan with San Jose. Around the same time, SVS&E decided to withdraw from its managing partnership, thus leaving AEG as the sole investor/operator of the club.

For the 2003 season, Yallop brought in some new players, notably Brian Ching, Brian Mullen and goalkeeper Pat Onstad. Despite a solid core unit of players, the Quakes were not an automatic shoe-in to claw their way back into another championship run. But come November, the team did exactly that.

THE GREATEST GAME IN MLS HISTORY

The date of November 9, 2003, will forever be etched in American soccer history as one of the greatest comebacks of all time, in any era, under any circumstances. With everything at stake, in a heated, bitter playoff match still recognized by many as the greatest game in MLS history, San Jose overturned a 4–0 deficit to eliminate the Los Angeles Galaxy at Spartan Stadium.

Mired by chilly weather, dark overhead clouds and eerie atmospherics, the match was the second of a two-game aggregate series. LA won the first match at home, 2–0, which meant the Quakes were already in the hole at the start of the second game at Spartan.

"We go down to LA…we got our asses handed to us, to be honest," Yallop said. "Two to zero, but it could have been more. We didn't play well. We didn't ever play well at the Home Depot Center."

During those days, LA and San Jose had the most bitter, intense rivalry in the league. Their playoff battles amplified the emotion even more.

"We didn't like each other," said Yallop. "I have a lot—a ton—of respect for Sigi [Schmid] and his teams, but our players didn't like their players… It was brewing."

By the time the second game got going in San Jose, LA scored twice in the first fifteen minutes, giving them a 4–0 lead on aggregate, so all hope seemed lost. LA, then the defending champs, hadn't allowed more than two goals in a game all season, and now the Quakes needed five.

But San Jose did not give up. In front of 14,145 fans, in a precursor to their "Never Say Die" tagline years later, the Quakes pulled off the impossible. They scored five unanswered goals, including Chris Roner's thrilling equalizer right at the ninety-minute mark and then a cinematic sudden-death-overtime winner by Rodrigo Faria. Choose your sport—American football, baseball, basketball, hockey or what have you—and pick your textbook postseason miracle comeback battle. This was Joe Montana entering the second half down 28–0 and then throwing five touchdowns to win the game. It was that kind of miracle. That's what happened.

Defender Jeff Agoos began the comeback with a set piece, curling a free kick into the net, cutting LA's lead to 2–1 and thus 4–1 on aggregate. Just before halftime, Donovan scored the Quakes' second goal of the match, tying the game at two and bringing the aggregate to 4–2. At that moment, what seemed hopeless at first was now, at least, well, imaginable. As the first half came to a close, the drama seemed unbearable for some, but Dayak claims that for him, the tipping point came when he saw a giant "We Believe" banner hanging in the south end of the stadium. "I'll never forget walking off the field," Dayak said. "I turned around and I saw it. It was huge, massive, all the way along the back. I walked into the locker room…I don't even remember Frank giving us a speech, because I remember getting up and saying, 'Guys, did you see that banner? That's what we need to do.'"

The team was already riled up. They were ready to go back out and get the job done in the second half. By the time Yallop did emerge for a pep talk, it was a no-brainer. "For me, that was the easiest halftime talk I've ever had," said Yallop. "[I said,] 'I'm telling you right now, guys, we score the next goal. They will buckle. They will. They have to. They're going to start hitting back, and then we're going to get on top of them. We've got to score early.'"

The pressure was so intense that Yallop and his goalkeeper coach, Tim Hanley, both took a quick nip of vodka and Red Bull before heading back out to the sidelines. They needed to mellow out. "I was shaking," recalled Yallop. "Tim's looking at me, and I was like, 'I need to calm down.' All the stuff going on…we just went, 'Hey, just take a little nip of vodka and Red Bull.' And we did just to calm our nerves."

When Jamil Walker scored the next Quakes goal, giving San Jose the lead at 3–2, they were still behind 4–3 on aggregate. The rest of the half unfolded with the fan noise growing louder and louder by the minute.

Even at ninety minutes, just about the end of regulation, many thought it couldn't, wouldn't or shouldn't happen. But when Richard Mulrooney sent in a cross from the corner and Chris Roner managed to get his head on the ball and put it behind keeper Kevin Hartman, tying the aggregate score at four, the resulting cacophony from 14,145 people sounded more like 100,000.

Despite the fact that I had grown up attending NASL matches, then worked in concession stands or drank in the crowd as a fan and now occupied the press box—for all practical purposes, spending a lifetime in that venue—at that moment, the noise erupting after that tying goal was the loudest I had ever heard in Spartan Stadium.

Then, in a play that can only be described as cinematic, Rodrigo Faria completed the comeback. The MLS Rookie of the Year for the NY/NJ MetroStars in 2001, Faria wound up with the Earthquakes in 2003 but made only seven appearances and hadn't even scored a goal until that point. Six minutes into overtime, Donovan slotted a pass to Faria at the top of the box. From there, Faria buried it past Hartman, cementing what is to this day the greatest comeback in MLS history.

After scoring the winner, Faria slid to the far corner, fell back onto his knees and looked up to the sky, apparently speaking to the Almighty. What looked like the entire San Jose franchise, from the field and the bench, dogpiled on top of him as he gushed with tears. The crowd erupted in a tumultuous rage of fanfare.

The view from the press box was borderline-mystical. Many in the crowd were either dressed in parkas or had one nearby, since it was supposed to rain that night. A dismal forecast had predicted a cold and wet evening. But during the game, rain did not arrive—that is, not until San Jose players jumped on top of Faria to celebrate. At that moment, it started drizzling, as if Mother Nature had deliberately waited until the game was over.

There was also a full moon that night. What was now the loudest crowd I'd ever heard at Spartan Stadium roared at the top of its collective lungs,

Rodrigo Faria after netting the winner in the greatest comeback in MLS history, 2003. *John Todd/ISI Photos; San Jose Earthquakes.*

and as the team dogpiled on top of Faria and nearly everyone in the press box also cheered, I looked southeast, diagonally across the stadium and up into a gunmetal sky. Just above the trees, the clouds slowly began to open like curtains on a stage, revealing the full moon for the first time all evening.

After the game, a battery of reporters, cameramen and even league executives filled the Quakes' locker room. Just about everyone of every age said it was the most spectacular match they'd ever experienced. Bruce Arena, then coach of the U.S. Men's National Team, was holding court, answering questions. "That was the best game this league's ever seen," he told us.

Rodrigo Faria heads up the ramp to the locker room after scoring the winning goal in the greatest comeback in MLS history. *John Todd/ISI Photos; San Jose Earthquakes.*

No one seemed to disagree. These days, objective observers shy away from using blanket-superlative phrases like "best game ever," but even now, in 2015, most would be hard-pressed to identify an **MLS** match any better than that one, especially since it was a playoff match between two bitter rivals.

Everything that most people want from the sporting experience unfolded that night: athleticism, drama, genius, teamwork, spirit, grit, endurance and a passionate home fan base of nuclear families, drunks, kids, adults, punks, executives and a zillion ethnicities from every part of the social spectrum, all rooting for the working-class underdog, replete with superstars and unsung nobodies all contributing to a systematic playoff-dismantling of a flashier, higher-profile opponent.

The following day, for an SI.com story, Arena told *Sports Illustrated* soccer guru Grant Wahl that such games gave him perfect opportunities to evaluate potential National Team players and how they performed under insane emotional pressure: "You'll see games like that in Europe. They're fast-paced, they're intense, and players are playing like it means something. If MLS went to a [single] table next year and had the top three or four teams get bonuses at the end of the year, every game would mean something. It would raise the level considerably."

Coaches, players and fans will never forget that match. Yallop, speaking in 2014, said he could still feel the cold weather and the eeriness of that evening. I could almost perceive him shivering over the phone. "I've not seen a better dramatic game than that, for what's at stake and what happened," said Yallop. "Here again, I'm not being biased with this, but I am. It was an incredible night. People still talk about it now."

San Jose Earthquakes versus Kansas City, MLS playoffs, November 15, 2003. *John Todd/ISI Photos; San Jose Earthquakes.*

Dayak says he made tons of friends among the fans that night. To this day, people still mention that game to him wherever he goes. "I can't tell you how many people have come to me and said, 'That game inspired me to coach' or 'to get my kids in soccer,'" he said.

After getting by Kansas City in yet another thrilling comeback in front of 16,108 fans at Spartan, the Quakes found their way into a second championship game in just three years. The stage was set.

The 2003 MLS Cup Final proved to be the perfect capper on Frank Yallop's first tenure with the club. The championship match was predetermined to unfold at the Home Depot Center, the LA Galaxy's brand-new stadium complex, built by AEG on the campus of California State University–Dominguez Hills (CSUDH) in Carson, about fifteen miles south of downtown Los Angeles. In a match that is still cited as one of the better MLS Cup finals, the Quakes defeated the Chicago Fire in a thrilling 4–2 match with several highlights. Landon Donovan scored twice, Chicago tallied on an own goal by the Quakes' Chris Roner and San Jose keeper Pat Onstad saved a penalty kick. Since the Home Depot Center had just opened earlier in the year, the San Jose Earthquakes became the first team ever to win an MLS Championship at that stadium.

At the time, I was still covering every Quakes match for the now-defunct SlideTackleMagazine.com and occasionally additional material for *Metro Silicon Valley*, but there was no travel budget, so I used frequent flier miles on Southwest to get to Los Angeles and then pay for a room in the Torrance Marriott, all without even renting a car. It was so pathetic—I had to bum a ride from the *Oakland Tribune*'s Dennis Miller just to get from the hotel to the stadium.

At the Home Depot Center, non-daily journalists for that match were stuck in what was referred to as the "auxiliary press box." Coincidentally, it was located just above sections 126 and 127, where a few hundred San Jose fans were sitting. It was not easy being an impartial, disconnected reporter, especially with those fans right below me, swilling beer, screaming and singing. I felt like writing a story with stolen language from quantum mechanics, one about how the observer is never separate from what's being observed.

With that game, under Frank Yallop and Dominic Kinnear, the Quakes won their second championship in three years. Johnny Moore, a 1974 NASL Quakes original, was still the team's GM. The lineage had finally come full circle. From 2001 to 2003, the Quakes were the best team in MLS, with a record of 41-25-18 over those three seasons.

In the press conference afterward, everyone seemed to already know that Yallop would soon accept a job with the Canadian National Team, enabling

The San Jose Earthquakes celebrating their second MLS Cup Championship, Home Depot Center, November 23, 2003. *John Todd/ISI Photos; San Jose Earthquakes.*

him to leave San Jose with a bang. Reporters grilled him about it as he sat there at the table, his kid in his arm, surrounded by Champagne and championship vibes.

"Frank, you can't keep dodging the question," one reporter said to him.

"Can I just enjoy this?" Yallop replied, with obvious annoyance in his voice.

After which he didn't answer. When all was said and done, I didn't ask anyone anything and eventually bummed a ride back to the Torrance Marriott from Jeff Carlisle, who then wrote for a website called QuakeMagic. com but who now writes for ESPN FC. It was the same hotel the team was staying in.

"The bus ride from the stadium to the hotel was fantastic," Kinnear recalled. "Everyone's singing and dancing. The only sad thing was, I had a real good feeling at that time that Frank was going to leave for Canada. It was a bit melancholy knowing that this incredible three-year ride was going to come to an end."

Reflecting on that championship run over fish and chips at Britannia Arms in 2014, Moore suggested that the 2003 Quakes squad was probably the highlight of the last forty years. And he's one to judge.

"That team that started in LA, that won the cup, was maybe the best Earthquake team ever put together," Moore said. "If you asked, 'How

The 2003 San Jose Earthquakes, MLS Cup champions. *John Todd/ISI Photos; San Jose Earthquakes.*

many National Team players were on that starting eleven?'—the answer was nine. We had nine out of eleven with National Team caps [for their respective countries]."

Following his second championship, Yallop eventually did return to his home country of Canada, officially resigning from the San Jose Earthquakes in December. It was not a simple decision, considering all the counter-interests. When recalling the move, he seemed to harbor mixed emotions, but he had no regrets. "It's bittersweet, because if I look back, I should have stayed in San Jose," Yallop said. "You make decisions, you live by them and you move on. After I did that, I saw that I wouldn't get another chance, maybe, to go to Canada. And I always wanted to do that."

After all, it was a different job entirely. As a National Team coach, Yallop ended up missing the day-to-day interactions with the players, but it was an opportunity he couldn't pass up.

"It was not easy," he admitted. "It was very difficult. Mixed emotions. All the players…I still have a fantastic relationship with. They've all remembered the good times, and those guys were fantastic to me and my staff. It's hard leaving that. Looking back, it would have been nice to see it through in San Jose and see what we could have done together. It is what it is."

Logically, Kinnear then ascended to the job of Quakes head coach, bringing in John Doyle as his assistant. Unfortunately, at the time, MLS still disavowed any possible connections to the NASL days. League executives never seemed to take history and lineage into account. Even with two championships in three years—better than anything accomplished by any San Jose team to that point—the league still seemed to downplay or de-emphasize the San Jose market. Even now with a head coach and assistant coach who'd grown up attending Quakes matches in the NASL days and then played together with the Blackhawks, plus a general manager who'd helped start the NASL club in 1974, AEG was already scheming to smash every fan's dreams by rebranding and/or relocating the team.

MOORE OR LESS

Many older Quakes fans leftover from the NASL days thought Johnny Moore represented exactly the type of character who should be in charge of the team, even if just in theory. He was the direct link to the very beginning of the club, and he now also had Silicon Valley business experience and a championship under his belt. And at the time, the San Jose Earthquakes were still the only MLS team exemplifying a direct connection to an original NASL moniker, which made them seem that much classier when compared to the rest of the league. As the fans saw it, Moore would be the one to finally sway the league executives into understanding the importance of history and heritage, as well as the emotional connections fans had with the history. He was someone who knew the myriad issues of the San Jose area, its geography and demographics. But AEG did not seem to express an interest in any of this.

"Early in 2004, I got a call from [AEG CEO] Tim Leiweke, saying he was going to sell the club to Club America [of Mexico City]," Moore told me. "And I said, 'What the hell are you talking about?' And he said, 'The president of Club America is going to be in San Jose tomorrow. They've got a game here, and I want you to meet him. But we're doing a deal, and we're going to sell it to Club America.'"

Everything Moore had spent his adult American life working toward—his club, the lineage he and Dick Berg helped launch at the San Jose Hyatt House in 1974—was now on the verge of being thrown out the window.

"To say I was pissed would be minimizing it," he recalled. "So that day, I fly to LA and find out that it's absolutely real—that he's trying to sell it, and it's going to go through. And I had just hired Dom [Kinnear], and Dom was at the pre-draft thing, and so now it's real. It's going to happen. So the Earthquake culture, what we built, it's suddenly going to become [another] Chivas USA."

At that time, MLS was already engaged in a wholly inane scheme to launch another Los Angeles–based franchise, Chivas USA, modeled after the real Chivas team in Guadalajara, one of the most storied Mexican clubs. Jorge Vergara, who had recently purchased the Guadalajara team, would lead the charge, and at least initially, the team was to function as an American satellite version of the real Chivas club. Since the real Chivas team prided itself on hiring only Mexican players and no foreigners, the initial discussions implied that this new satellite version would operate under the same philosophy—that is, it would prioritize Mexican or Mexican American players. Even before Chivas USA was officially announced later that year, the entire idea stunk of bumbling sports executives hopelessly trying to pander to the Latino community of Los Angeles.

The initial rumblings with Club America (Chivas's archrival in Mexico) suggested exactly the same, with leaks in the press from Club America's owner insinuating that he would take over the San Jose Earthquakes and rebrand the team as a similarly extracurricular Mexican experiment. A dumber idea could not have been possible, and Moore did not want the San Jose Earthquakes tradition he had helped launch twenty-nine years earlier morphing into anything of the sort.

"Chivas USA in Los Angeles was a bad bet," Moore told me in the summer of 2014, reflecting on those events of ten years earlier. "I felt it was the wrong way to go. If somebody wanted to have a Scottish team, so be it. But don't turn my San Jose Earthquakes into some kind of a foreign team and throw all its history away. That's not where I'm from. It's not what I do. So, needless to say, I resigned."

After flying back up to San Jose over the weekend, Moore broke it to his office staff on Monday morning, telling them he simply would not be part of any scenario that destroyed San Jose Earthquakes history. He also speculated that his resignation might throw enough of a wrench into the negotiations with Club America to force them to ask AEG for a better deal, given the bad press emerging from his resignation. He told his staff they would now probably have the rest of the 2004 season to find a new owner for the club, hopefully someone local, someone who valued the long San Jose Earthquakes history. He wished the staff good luck and remained on the periphery during the upcoming two seasons.

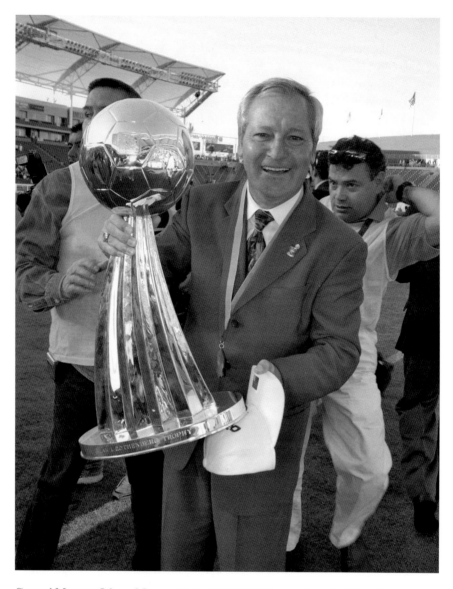

General Manager Johnny Moore with the 2003 MLS Cup trophy at the Home Depot Center. *John Todd/ISI Photos; San Jose Earthquakes*.

After all was said and done, AEG did not end up doing a deal with Club America. Instead, Leiweke came to San Jose for a press conference at the Fairmont Hotel on January 27, 2004, to install Alexi Lalas as the Quakes' president and general manager. The former 1994 World Cup star and LA

Galaxy defender, who was part of the squad just eliminated by the Quakes two months earlier in the greatest-ever MLS comeback, was now in charge of the team. Lalas, along with his acoustic guitar, would then move into the new Quakes offices at North Almaden and St. John in downtown San Jose, offices for which Johnny Moore had just signed the lease but never got a chance to move into.

At the press conference, Leiweke stressed that AEG was committed to the Quakes "this year," meaning 2004. More than once, he emphasized the words "this year" at the podium, suggesting that something was definitely up and that the team probably wouldn't be under AEG's stewardship in 2005.

As a result, San Jose played the entire 2004 season against a looming backdrop—that of whether AEG was going to relocate the team somewhere else. Houston came into the mix as the city with the highest television ratings for any market without a team. As the season wore on, it became clear that AEG was looking at Houston or San Antonio as the future home for the San Jose Earthquakes. All year, it seemed certain, but then it didn't. And then it did, and then it didn't. Nevertheless, Kinnear and Doyle soldiered on, retaining almost all of the 2003 championship team for 2004. As the season evolved, though, the team became plagued by injuries and National Team call-ups. After sneaking into the playoffs, the Quakes were eliminated by Kansas City in the first round.

But throughout 2004, as inklings of AEG's machinations began to solidify, a diehard group of Quakes fans decided they were not going to simply sit around and let their team be whisked away to the Lone Star State. A tightknit band of thirty-somethings, including several born and raised in the San Jose area and who'd grown up attending NASL matches at Spartan Stadium, started orchestrating a massive, unprecedented outreach to find a local owner for the team. A close-knit grassroots effort unlike anything seen before in professional sports began to materialize.

CHAPTER 8

WILL DRUM FOR STADIUM

In the spring of 2004, a group of local fans began to stage meetings at the Britannia Arms Pub in downtown San Jose to talk about how they could save the Earthquakes from moving. Colin McCarthy, by day an attorney at Robinson & Wood Inc., moonlighted as president of Club Quake, the team's booster organization. Taking the lead to organize a new effort to help save the team, McCarthy stepped down from Club Quake in order to found a new organization, eventually called Soccer Silicon Valley (SSV), a street-level grassroots operation. Another attorney, Don Gagliardi, approached him and became the number-two person on board. Lifelong fan John Jussen then joined them, as did graphic designer and journalist Jay Hipps, plus locals Mike Turco and Carol Vartuli-Marin.

Tony Huston, now also in his thirties, initially began operating on his own, collecting e-mails and contact info, but since he had similar ideas in mind, the group invited him to participate. Distraught at the potential of the Quakes dying yet again, Huston was frustrated and still harbored memories from when the Quakes folded the first time around. "I was pissed like a lot of other fans were," said Huston. "So I became very reactionary. And I was like, 'Screw this. I'm not going through this again.'"

In the subsequent months, the members of SSV put in massive hours strategizing, studying up on the sports business industry, familiarizing themselves with local politics, learning about stadium construction, reaching out to potential investors and putting in tons of work on top of their full-time jobs. Each one of them brought a different skill set to

Guy Gayle pounding his drum at the rally to save the San Jose Earthquakes, Plaza de Cesar Chavez, San Jose, August 20, 2004. *Joe Santos*.

the table, whether it was corporate presentation skills, public relations, litigation expertise, graphic design or just plain passionate, never-say-die fandom. All of this led up to a daring idea: stage a high-profile August rally at Plaza de Cesar Chavez in downtown San Jose and tell the world to help save this team.

"We knew we had to do something big," Huston said. "We were just a group of individuals trying to get people's attention, so I thought what we did was rather bold, actually. We decided, 'Hey, we're going to have a rally and make people realize there is passion here for this team.'"

Approximately two thousand fans showed up to the rally on August 20, 2004, including civic leaders, real estate impresarios, high-tech entrepreneurs, the entire current San Jose Earthquakes team, former players from decades earlier and even Krazy George. The event succeeded at raising awareness and generating publicity, with many others subsequently jumping on board to help with tasks related to finding local investors. The fan base mobilized, and word spread around the league that a massive effort was underway to save the San Jose Earthquakes.

At the rally, McCarthy took the microphone and shouted, "Instead of Raider Nation, it's going to be Earthquake Planet!" Others who spoke included Alexi Lalas, who introduced the entire 2004 team on the stage. Former general manager and NASL-era Quake Johnny Moore also

Johnny Moore speaking at the rally to save the Quakes, Plaza de Cesar Chavez, San Jose. *Joe Santos.*

introduced many players from the 1970s, who were in town for an official thirtieth anniversary reunion of the inaugural 1974 team. And that weekend, the 2004 team donned red throwback jerseys—in homage to the NASL era—during their home match against Dallas.

The celebration did not go entirely unscathed, however. One day before the rally, on August 19, in a series of private and presumably preemptive meetings carrying all the intrigue of a spy novel, Tim Leiweke of AEG showed up to San Jose along with then-COO Scott Blackmun to inform the entire team that it would soon be moved to Texas. That meeting took place at the Hilton San Jose & Towers, adjacent to the McEnery Convention Center. Later that morning, Leiweke and Blackmun led a second meeting at the Earthquakes offices with the founding members of SSV. In that meeting, AEG said, as it had in the team meeting, that the Quakes were headed to Texas.

If one looks at those two encounters as a home-and-away aggregate series, AEG might have won the first meeting, but at least according to the recollections of SSV members, AEG might not have won the second meeting. Questions were raised, propositions were put on the table and the members of SSV actually asked Leiweke to give them a month to find a new owner/operator for the team. Leiweke agreed, and AEG eventually promised in writing not to sell the team out from underneath everyone during those thirty days. AEG even supplied SSV with LA Galaxy financial data, season ticket information and other background materials necessary to include in any pitch made by SSV to potential investors—not something C-level sports executives are prone to do for just any clown on the street.

What's more, in that same meeting, the members of SSV, with Gagliardi leading the charge, made an audacious demand: all records, colors and statistics should remain in San Jose if the team relocates.

Gagliardi, an attorney specializing in intellectual property law, is known in San Jose for his passionate soccer fandom, his explosive determination and for being one who simply will not accept "no" for an answer. When recalling that meeting, Gagliardi said he was "forceful" in demanding that if AEG did ultimately move the team, all Earthquakes statistics and brand components must remain in San Jose, should the city ever get another MLS team. "I modeled this specifically after the Cleveland Browns," Gagliardi recalled. "I had that in mind. [I said to Leiweke], 'If you move the team, we get to keep the colors, the trophies, all the records, everything, here.' And Leiweke said, 'Yes, if we move the team, you will have that.' He made that pledge...and later honored it, so he deserves credit for that. Leiweke made that promise, and he honored it. But if we hadn't asked, it wouldn't have happened."

Huston agreed: "Collectively, we all sat there and said, 'This is what's going to happen. This is our stuff, this is our property. It doesn't belong to the league. This is our history, and it's going to stay here whether they like it or not.' And Don, being the passionate guy that he is, he took the lead and laid down the demands."

Adding that it's always smarter to let a lawyer argue such things, Huston continued: "We all sat around the table, and when everything went down, we all kinda said, 'Fuck this—this is our team, these are our colors, this is our history. We're keeping it. It's our shit.' And when you get Don excited, you can't stop him."

Again, sometimes it's the tiny decisions that dramatically reshape the future, before anyone even realizes it. One can only speculate as to how MLS would now be different had San Jose been shafted out of its two championship trophies, all its records and its moniker. But MLS spokesman Dan Courtemanche, who was with the league at the time, said no one had a problem with San Jose hanging on to its records. "At no point did I hear anyone object to the recommendation to continue to keep the records in San Jose," said Courtemanche. "And I do remember that Lamar Hunt was pretty vocal with saying the records should stay—à la the Cleveland Browns—and that that was a smart move. And ultimately it was Commissioner Garber's decision to move forward with that process."

The day following the rally, the Quakes wore throwback NASL jerseys for their match that Saturday and gave their best performance of the 2004 season, trouncing Dallas 3–0. Old-timers from the NASL played a short reunion game beforehand. And during the pregame lineup, the MLS Quakes stunned the crowd by unfurling a long banner that read, "Keep Us in San Jose"—a surprise stunt devised by three players: Troy Dayak, Ronnie Ekelund and Jeff Agoos. As the team stood there on the field, holding that banner, the unprecedented gesture drew a standing ovation from the entire crowd at Spartan Stadium.

Dayak said the stunt arose partly from his own memories of scoring the winning goal against Miami in the playoffs three years earlier when both San Jose and Miami had been on the league's potential chopping block for contraction. Remembering the miserable uncertainty of the 2001 situation, he didn't want to go through that again. "We were just trying to think of any way possible to keep us here," Dayak said. "And at that time, we didn't have social media and Facebook and Instagram and SnapChat and all that stuff. I guess the best way to do it was to let people know that we wanted to stay."

As the days unfolded, the members of SSV, intentionally or unintentionally, became the de facto go-between for the fans and possibly even the players. Everyone seemed anxious for updates about was being done to stop the team from moving to Texas. At the time, Jussen owned Time Deli at the corner of Bascom and San Carlos in San Jose's Burbank neighborhood. "Some of the Earthquakes players would come over to the deli every Friday to try and

The author's *Metro Silicon Valley* story on the efforts of Soccer Silicon Valley to find a new owner for the San Jose Earthquakes. *Author's collection.*

hear what was going on," said Jussen. "They wanted to know if there was any news or anything like that—especially Craig Waibel, Brian Ching and Brian Mullen. These guys all wanted to stay."

In September, AEG eventually extended the thirty-day window, but with only one potential lead investor, Tony Amanpour, failing to come through on his promises, not much could be accomplished. Several other interested parties, including the San Jose Sharks, began to kick the tires on a regular basis, but no one group had enough wherewithal to guarantee a path toward a new stadium of any sort.

Ultimately, it can be understood that the success of the rally and the massive public awareness it raised, as well as the highly intricate network of correspondence orchestrated by SSV in its outreach to potential investors, is at least partly what bought the Earthquakes another season in 2005. AEG did not end up moving the team following the 2004 season, and on November 9, GM Alexi Lalas held a makeshift press conference in the Earthquakes offices at 100 North Almaden Avenue to announce that 2005 season tickets were now on sale. The conference featured reporters—four of us—sitting around a table upstairs with Lalas while he gave us the lowdown. No one else showed up.

CHAPTER 9

ABANDONMENT ISSUES

In 2005, despite the looming backdrop of what AEG was up to, Dominic Kinnear led the Earthquakes to their best season ever, statistically speaking. The squad won the MLS Supporters' Shield for the best record in the entire league that year (18-4-10, sixty-four points), setting a league record for the fewest losses in a season—a record that still stands today. That year, the team also became the first club in MLS history to finish an entire season unbeaten at home (9-0-7). For me, it brought back haunting memories of the 1983 NASL side, one that also went undefeated at home, just as that league was beginning to circle the drain and just before the NASL Quakes franchise soon folded for good. As a result of San Jose's stellar achievements, Kinnear was named the 2005 MLS Coach of the Year, just as the Quakes' Don Popovic was the 1983 NASL Coach of the Year. In 2005, it seemed like history really was repeating itself—in eerie fashion.

However, even though the 2005 squad set many other team records that season, they accomplished everything without Landon Donovan, who, after completing his four-year loan, returned to Bayer Leverkusen in Germany following the 2004 season. When that adventure did not work out, Donovan promptly returned to MLS, opting to play for the Quakes' bitter rival, Los Angeles, at the beginning of the 2005 season. With the Quakes' future completely up in the air, Donovan chose to be nearer to his home turf and his family, with whom he was very close. In other words, he chose personal happiness over a sketchy, uncertain career situation, which is what most adults would do. However, this did not sit well with many Earthquakes

San Jose's Brian Ching takes on the New England Revolution in 2005. *John Todd/ISI Photos; San Jose Earthquakes.*

fans, who viewed it in the same way that Barcelona fans viewed Luis Figo's traitorous move to Real Madrid.

Unlike in Barcelona, though, Quakes fans did not throw a severed pig's head at Donovan when he first came back to Spartan Stadium with the Galaxy on June 25, 2005. Instead, they constructed a goofy life-sized piñata in his likeness, replete with receding hairline, and bashed the hell out of it in the parking lot beforehand. John Jussen, now with a seven-year-old son himself, played a key role in the operation.

At the tailgate before the game, numerous fans and their kids took shots at the piñata, finally breaking it open. While other kids went straight for the scattered contents, Jussen's son Ray immediately grabbed the decapitated head and held it up for the *San Jose Mercury-News* photographer who was waiting in the wings to capture the action. "The head rolled, and all the kids ran for the candy, but Ray, he grabbed Landon's head," recalled Jussen with a laugh. "I don't know what prompted him to do that, but he held it up in sort of a *Lord of the Flies* moment. He was very proud of himself."

Some condemned the charade, while others said it was harmless. But the preparation of the piñata made the *Mercury-News* days before the game even started, which then triggered ESPN to run pregame footage of kids smashing it to smithereens.

And at the start of the game, in protest of Donovan's move to Los Angeles, as his name came up during the lineup announcements, at least one-third of the 15,917 in attendance stood up and turned their backs in choreographed fashion. During the game, thousands booed him whenever he touched the ball. Others hung anti-Landon banners all throughout the stadium—stuff like "No Respect for the Traitor Quitter" and "Landon Judas Donovan." One banner was even directed to the ownership group itself: "AEG: Anti-Earthquakes Group." It was San Jose's mini-version of Camp Nou in Barcelona when Figo came back with Real Madrid, except the pigs did not fly.

In the subsequent days, the LA-based media seemed to take deep offense at how harshly Landon was treated. But in my opinion, the San Jose fans exhibited the truest form of raw passion for their team. The stadium environment that night—banners, traitorous accusations and the loudest boos ever at Spartan that I can recall, plus noise, confetti and biblical references—felt like what I imagined a true long-standing football rivalry was probably like anywhere else in the world. And this was 2005, before Seattle, Portland or Vancouver had come into the league and before the Cascadia rivalry went on to eclipse everything else. And with all due respect to the LA media who felt insulted, it wasn't as bad as having a pig's head thrown at you.

That night, the passionate environment got into the Galaxy's head, and the Quakes won 3–0, thanks in part to two own goals by Los Angeles. Donovan was never a factor in the match. The next day, the *Mercury-News* featured Jussen's son Ray on the front page of the sports section, in color, holding the decapitated head from the Donovan piñata.

Predictably, none of this passionate rivalry had any effect on AEG, which continued putting touches on a Quakes relocation to Texas. The members of SSV still held regular conversations with potential investor/operators, including the San Jose Sharks and even a representative from Ajax America, but all those involved were essentially kicking the tires without committing to anything long term. The buzzards began to circle the franchise, just as they had in 1984.

Unfortunately for San Jose, Landon and the Galaxy got the last laugh in dramatic fashion. Even though the Quakes were easily the league's best team during the regular season, the Galaxy, after barely even making the playoffs, knocked San Jose out of those playoffs in the first round. And it was Landon who helped seal San Jose's fate.

The conference semifinals were played in a two-game home-and-away aggregate series, just like in the UEFA Champions League. But even though the Earthquakes had sailed to the league's best record that year, nearly twenty points ahead of the Galaxy, the SoCal team prevailed, taking the series 4–2 on aggregate. LA won the first game at the Home Depot Center, 3–1, with Donovan scoring two of the goals. The second match at Spartan Stadium brought back intense memories of the legendary comeback game two years earlier, but LA would not let itself get embarrassed this time around. The game ended in a 1–1 draw, and the Quakes' 2005 Supporters' Shield season—to this day the team's best-ever campaign—was now over.

After the match, the crowd of 17,824 exited the stands, all of them pretty much aware that the franchise might be over as well. It was probably the last San Jose Earthquakes match for good, as AEG was ready to pull the trigger any moment and move the team to Houston. Only those in extreme denial still refused to believe it was going to happen.

Following that playoff loss, Tony Huston says he was the last person left in the stands. Sitting there all by himself, even after his family had ascended the stairs and made their way out, he contemplated his whole life's worth of dedication to supporting the San Jose Earthquakes. He felt like a balloon with all its air squeezed out. "I cried that day, just as I did that day when Peter Bridgwater was out on the field [in 1984]," Huston recalled. "I remember that last game [in 2005], I sat in the stadium until security kicked me out. Actually, security told me to get out three times."

But Huston wouldn't leave at first. Suffering through the NASL Earthquakes' demise twenty-one years earlier as a kid was bad enough for him, but now it was happening all over again. Just as he had recalled "Chariots of Fire" playing during Bridgwater's speech, he remembered the music when the MLS San Jose Earthquakes ended this time around as he sat there, refusing to leave Spartan Stadium. "They were playing that Hawaiian guy, Israel Kamakawiwo'ole... the song was 'Somewhere Over the Rainbow,'" Huston told me. "There was nobody in the stadium. Alexi Lalas was down on the field with some kid, and I wanted to go down there and call him a prick. And as I walked out of the stadium, I was like, 'This is crap, you know? This is crap.' I wanted to bring my kids to come watch the Quakes, just like my dad did. [Now] I didn't think I was going to have that opportunity."

During those years, MLS was roughly half the size it is now. San Jose and Los Angeles were the only West Coast teams, and their rivalry can be understood as the most authentic, homegrown, bitter, vicious and truly passionate one of its kind in the league at that time. It was not a hokey, ersatz, league-manufactured rivalry like the Galaxy/Chivas USA derby that would later emerge. Instead, it was the real thing, right down to the very sentiments of the fans, coaches and players. These were two teams that truly did not like each other, all of which bore fruit via alternating championships. The Quakes defeated the Galaxy to win the title in 2001. The following year, the Galaxy likewise won its first title, and then in 2003, the Quakes won again after knocking the Galaxy from the playoffs in the greatest comeback in league history. Then, in 2005, Los Angeles snuck into the playoffs and eliminated San Jose before going on to win the title. As one might witness in several other homegrown rivalries throughout the world, LA was the flashier, richer, flagship franchise the league always seemed to prefer, while San Jose was the ignored bunch, the underdogs and a true working-class group of guys.

"We were considered the redheaded stepchild," Dayak told me, adding that AEG, which owned both teams in the end, played blatant favorites. The Quakes were the ones cast aside, the afterthought, while the LA Galaxy team was the golden child, the prodigy team. Los Angeles had a brand-new stadium, multiple training facilities, turf fields, locker rooms and hospital-style MRI machines. In San Jose's case, the team's training sessions exemplified the polar opposite. Quakes players had to drive to Spartan Stadium and enter those same 1950s-era locker rooms to change into their gear, get their cleats, get taped or get any treatment they needed. Then they had to get into their own cars and drive twenty miles down the freeway to practice on the fields at West Valley College in Saratoga, with no showers and no bathrooms. Afterward, the team then had to get back into their own cars, sometimes soaking wet, muddy and sweating, just to drive twenty miles back to Spartan Stadium in order to shower, get treatment, get cleaned up and then go back home and do it all over again the next day.

"But it helped build our character," Dayak said. "We never complained about it, and it was part of the heart and soul of who we were and part of why we were so successful and defiant."

For the fans, to see such a passionate rivalry suddenly get yanked away for no logical reason was devastating. For the fans who grew up with the NASL team, those who'd suffered through a similar Quakes death before, the grief was twofold. "It sucks to lose something that you truly care about, that you're passionate about," Huston told me. "But to get it back and then lose it again is even worse. Especially if you've put in so many years of effort…you've put certain things, relationships, on hold. It was heartbreaking."

On November 15, 2005, MLS commissioner Don Garber announced that the MLS board of directors had voted to let AEG relocate the team. One month later, AEG pulled the trigger, officially announcing Houston as the new home of the Earthquakes. Kinnear and whoever on his staff wanted to go with him were given a moment's notice to pack up their operation. After half a lifetime's worth of hanging out at Spartan Stadium, after growing up at NASL Quakes matches, after playing both as a kid and professionally on that field and then after assistant-coaching the Quakes to two championships and subsequently coaching the team to its best-ever record, Kinnear was now contractually obligated to move to Houston if he still wanted to coach in Major League Soccer.

"At that time, it was a tough one," Kinnear said. "I changed my mind more times than I care to remember. Just leaving home, leaving family and moving to a place. I had no idea what Houston was about at all."

Kinnear said he and his staff were in the Quakes compound at St. John and North Almaden when the suits came in and broke the news: "I just remember we had a meeting at the offices down there, and they just came in and said, 'The team's moving to Houston.' And I was asked to get some good clothes together and fly to Houston…We attended a press conference the next morning, we flew back to San Jose and then it was a complete scramble to get ourselves ready for the next year."

Joe Cannon, who by then was manning the posts for Colorado, recalls more than a tinge of heartbreak upon hearing about the relocation. After all the different phases—the league initially owning the team, then the Kraft Group and subsequently the San Jose Sharks operating the franchise and now AEG announcing that Texas would be the team's new home—Cannon said he was distraught. "I felt like it was a big mistake," Cannon told me. "I just felt like it was the wrong decision. I just felt like the ownership groups of the past just never gave it a 100 percent chance. They never said, 'Hey, we're going to see if this thing can really work.' I think it was something that you really couldn't understand. You did in a business sense, but you didn't in the sense that you just felt like nobody was giving them a chance."

The situation was not without hope, however. When announcing the team's relocation, Garber said that San Jose would retain the rights to the Earthquakes name, logo and colors, as well as its entire MLS history of statistics, records and championship trophies, all to be reinstated should a new team return to San Jose. The City of San Jose had even signed a letter of intent to do just that, Garber said—to host a new, permanent version of the San Jose Earthquakes once a new owner and stadium could be realistically envisioned.

This meant that the Houston team would begin as an expansion franchise, starting at zero, and that the two Earthquakes championship trophies, as

One fan's homemade shirt after AEG relocated the San Jose Earthquakes to Houston. *Author's collection.*

well as the Supporters' Shield trophy, would remain in San Jose. Houston would not get to claim those records or trophies. They belonged to San Jose. The efforts of SSV had paid off.

Also in that same announcement, Garber said conversations were already underway with real estate magnate and Oakland A's owner Lew Wolff about the possibility of taking out an option to bring the Quakes back. On one hand, it was face-saving claptrap by Garber, for certain, but Wolff did indeed have decades-long roots and connections in San Jose. He'd built hotels and mid-rise office towers in San Jose going back to the 1960s. If anyone could navigate the political and real estate quagmires of the city, it was Wolff.

CHAPTER 10
EXPANSION RATE

The conversations with Wolff eventually paid off. Along with his partner in the A's ownership group, Gap Clothing heir John Fisher, Wolff took out an option on May 24, 2006, to resurrect a Quakes team and re-crystallize the history, provided a path toward building a new stadium could seriously emerge. They officially exercised that option on July 18, 2007. Three months later, John Doyle came on board as general manager, followed by the return of Frank Yallop in November. Different layers of multi-era Quakes history were thus cemented from the top on down.

But the coaching scenario almost could have had a different outcome altogether. After relocating to Houston, Kinnear had gone on to win the next two MLS championships in 2006 and 2007 with, for all practical purposes, the same former-Earthquakes team. According to Kinnear, when the late Doug Hamilton was helping put together Kinnear's future contract as the team moved from San Jose to Houston, he asked if Kinnear wanted a particular clause included—one that would allow him to return as San Jose's coach should a new franchise emerge. "He was the one doing my contract," Kinnear recalled. "I said I would like this amount of years, etc., etc., and he said—and God rest him because he's not alive anymore—he said, 'Do you want me to put a clause in there that will allow you to go back to San Jose if they bring the team back?' And I said to Doug, 'Doug, I appreciate the offer, but no. I don't want to be thinking about going back to San Jose all the time. I want to just concentrate on being here.' And he was cool with that."

Coach Frank Yallop with General Manager John Doyle. *John Todd/ISI Photos; San Jose Earthquakes.*

It made sense because no one could have predicted how quickly the Quakes would reemerge. So when Lew Wolff exercised the option just less than twenty-four months after the team had relocated, Kinnear nearly kicked himself for turning down that offer: "When I heard two years later that the Earthquakes were coming back, the first thing I thought [to myself] was, 'You son of a gun—what were you thinking?'"

Yallop and Kinnear were and still are close pals, so Kinnear said there were no hard feelings. All was good. "I have some good friends in soccer, and I've had great friends in soccer," said Kinnear. "And Frank is a great friend of mine, as everyone knows. I was a little bit jealous because he got to go back, but I don't think they could have found a better guy."

Once the Quakes did come back, however, the path toward a new stadium did not materialize overnight. The team resumed play in 2008, but due to conflicting views of the future between the new ownership group and San Jose State University, the team would no longer call Spartan Stadium home. The Quakes opted for the even more decrepit facility of Buck Shaw Stadium at Santa Clara University, where they would play their games for the next seven seasons. Since Buck Shaw held fewer than 10,000 people, the Quakes eventually had to pay for extra makeshift seats and grandstands to make the venue look something remotely close to professional. Even then, the capacity became a timid 10,500, the smallest facility in the league by far.

From 2008 to 2011, San Jose reached the playoffs only once, in 2010, and even then they barely squeezed through. In the first round, led by former U.S.

Norwich legend Darren Huckerby came to play for the Earthquakes in 2008. *John Todd/ISI Photos; San Jose Earthquakes.*

Chris Wondolowski (right) celebrating after a goal at Buck Shaw Stadium. *John Todd/ISI Photos; San Jose Earthquakes.*

National Team star Bobby Convey, the Quakes upset the higher-profile New York Red Bulls in a two-game series before falling 1–0 to the Colorado Rapids in a very dismal semifinal match. In the end, the Quakes were one goal away from the 2010 MLS Cup Final, but without their own stadium, the newly resurrected franchise still seemed to lumber on in perpetual limbo mode.

The year 2010 also marked a breakout season for Danville native Chris Wondolowski, whom the Quakes had acquired from Houston halfway through the previous season. "Wondo," as he came to be known, led the league in scoring that year, earning the MLS Golden Boot. During the next few seasons, Wondo became the team's first primary visible poster boy since the days of Landon Donovan.

As the new stadium continued to drag on through city council meetings, revisions, neighbor complaints, designs and updates, the Quakes continued playing their home games at Buck Shaw. Originally, no one thought the team would endure for a total of seven seasons at the venue, but the new stadium effort required a few extra years' worth of hoops to jump through before the groundbreaking finally occurred on October 21, 2012. For the groundbreaking celebration, the Quakes staged an event somewhere between old-school performance art and sheer propaganda. The team ordered thousands of blue shovels just for the occasion and invited whoever wanted to show up and help dig. After all was said and done, 6,256 fans had

A total of 6,256 fans digging for two straight minutes to set a Guinness World Record for the largest participatory groundbreaking ceremony of all time, October 2012. *John Todd/ISI Photos; San Jose Earthquakes.*

dug for two straight minutes to set a Guinness World Record for the largest participatory groundbreaking ceremony of all time.

Located right across from Mineta San Jose International Airport, the eighteen-thousand-capacity stadium broke ground just as the Quakes were completing a multiple-record-setting Supporters' Shield season, their second in franchise history. It was a wild emotional ride if ever there was one.

The 2012 season, which finally seemed like a championship season of old, energized a frustrated fan base by ratcheting up the drama more than ever before. Chris Wondolowski emerged as the league's leading scorer yet again, this time with a whopping twenty-seven goals on the year, which tied Roy Lassiter's long-standing MLS record. On the whole, the team led the league with seventy-two goals on the season, a franchise record and the third-highest total in league history, while finishing with a 19-6-9 record (sixty-six points), also the best in the league. In the process, San Jose's attacking trio of Wondolowski, Alan Gordon (thirteen goals) and Steven Lenhart (ten goals) scored fifty of those seventy-two goals. By comparison, the team with the second-best record, Sporting Kansas City, scored only forty-two goals on the season. Pundits almost unanimously predicted and/or hailed Los Angeles, Real Salt Lake and Seattle to repeat their 2011 achievements as the three strongest teams in the league, but in 2012, the Quakes defeated each of those teams twice.

Chris Wondolowski at Buck Shaw Stadium. *Michael Pimentel/ISI Photos; San Jose Earthquakes.*

What's more, the 2012 season was marked by a series of mind-boggling comeback matches in the closing minutes of stoppage time. In no fewer than nine instances, the Quakes scored past the ninety-minute mark, with five of those occurrences resulting in wins. Fans throughout the league have argued ever since about whether it was all just luck, but in any case, nothing

The San Jose Earthquakes winning the Supporters' Shield for the league's best record, 2012. *John Todd/ISI Photos; San Jose Earthquakes.*

of the sort had ever happened in the history of MLS. No team had come from behind to tie and/or win a total of nine games in post-ninety-minute stoppage time during one season.

The game-by-game comebacks in the waning moments seemed to mirror on a micro level the larger story of the entire Earthquakes saga. From the very beginning, in 1974, league executives hadn't even wanted San Jose. Then the team exploded out of the gate with the league's best attendance averages, defeating Pelé and the Cosmos not once but twice. Then the whole league collapsed, only to resurface in various forms until MLS, when a series of absentee owners disregarded the team as an afterthought all over again. And yet here they were in 2012, once again refusing to die, leading the league and humiliating opponent after opponent in stoppage time.

The comeback phenomenon accelerated new team branding efforts in the process, albeit goofy ones. The Quakes started calling themselves the Goonies. The aggressive and physical duo of Lenhart and Gordon became known as the Bash Brothers, heisted from Oakland A's sluggers Mark McGwire and Jose Canseco, who had powered that team in the late

Simon Dawkins, on loan from Tottenham Hotspur, helped propel the Quakes to the 2012 Supporters' Shield. *John Todd/ISI Photos; San Jose Earthquakes.*

1980s. In the former case, it sounded more like a roller derby concoction than a soccer nickname. It was hokey, but the fans ate it up.

In any event, the Quakes rolled to their best record ever, rallying their fans like never before. And 2012's success was not entirely due to comebacks and the scoring prowess of Wondolowski, Lenhart and Gordon. Englishman Simon Dawkins, on loan from Tottenham Hotspur, and Honduran Marvin Chavez provided unpredictable dribbling prowess, confidence on the ball and creative midfield supplements that tended to break games open and cause serious problems for any opposing squad.

Unfortunately for the Quakes, their old archenemies from SoCal eliminated them in the end. Exactly like in 2005, when San Jose finished with the league's best record and the Los Angeles Galaxy snuck into the playoffs at the bottom and final slot, history soon repeated itself. In the first round of the playoffs, the two rivals met, and things did not bode well for San Jose. Although the Quakes won the first game of the aggregate series 1–0 at the Home Depot Center, they lost the second one at home, 3–1. The team's record-setting 2012 campaign was over.

Even as 2013 unfolded, the stadium effort was put on hold one last time, as excavation crews hit some underground bunkers on the stadium site, which was formerly occupied by the FMC Corporation. As a result, opening was delayed until 2015. That was not the only surprise, however.

On June 7, 2013, an official team announcement declared that the Quakes and Yallop had "mutually agreed" to part ways. At first, no one anywhere seemed to accept such a simplified explanation. As a result, rampant speculation rippled across the Quakes universe, and every frustration already percolating throughout the fan base came to the surface. Had other teams figured the Quakes out, leaving San Jose with no strategy? Did the absence of a replacement for Simon Dawkins leave a gaping hole in the offense? Who was responsible for that decision and others? Did Yallop finally walk out over some final straw of some sort? Or did the team prematurely cut him loose, as other impatient squads had done in similar situations? Even though the team had started the 2013 campaign rather poorly—at that point, a 3-6-6 record hardly seemed adequate following a league-leading season—the announcement had nevertheless stunned everyone.

In a 2014 conversation with me, Yallop would not go into specifics, but he explained that after a meeting with GM John Doyle and President Dave Kaval, all three of them arrived at a mutual conclusion: "Me and Dave and John chatted—and it was by mutual consent, by the way. It wasn't like I was fired or I quit. It was a conversation—and this is the truth—where we talked it out and just felt that as we're looking at each other, it's like, 'Let's end it. Let's end the relationship.' Everyone agreed on it."

As a result, the team appointed assistant coach Mark Watson as its new interim chief. After achieving an impressive run for the rest of 2013, the Earthquakes finished with a 14-11-9 record, which tied them with Colorado for the final playoff spot in the Western Conference. But due to the resulting goals-for tiebreaker, San Jose did not make it through.

The successful post-Yallop 2013 run was enough to keep Watson on the payroll, so the Quakes entered the following season just as grand-scale

San Jose's Chris Wondolowski and Victor Bernardez at Buck Shaw Stadium. *John Todd/ISI Photos; San Jose Earthquakes.*

plans for a fortieth anniversary year (1974–2014) were about to explode. To highlight the anniversary era, an uncanny series of developments in 2014, unpredictable by anyone, was about to unfold, bringing the entire Earthquakes saga full circle in borderline-mystical fashion.

CHAPTER 11

ANNIVERSARY EFFECTS

On January 30, 2014, the San Jose Earthquakes officially kicked off their fortieth anniversary year—their final campaign before the debut of their new stadium—by unveiling a new logo and brand concept as part of an elaborate and emotional public bash in San Pedro Square Market at the corner of St. John and North San Pedro Streets in downtown San Jose. Ironically, one of the market buildings, at Almaden and St. John, was formerly the 2005-era Quakes front offices before the team moved to Houston.

A relatively new urban space filled with upmarket artisan foodstuffs, local independent retail and event spaces spilling out into the local urban fabric, the San Pedro Square Market sits primarily on land owned by former mayor McEnery's family for generations and had emerged a few years earlier as a way to highlight San Jose's oft-ignored but most historical buildings: the Peralta Adobe and the Fallon House. On January 30, the market seemed tailored to function as a backdrop for the fortieth anniversary of San Jose's original yet oft-ignored pro sports franchise.

At least a few thousand folks jammed the streets outside for the party. While ambling through the masses during a brief conversation with the author, former mayor McEnery even compared and contrasted himself to Krazy George. "We're from the same era," McEnery told me. "But he was never crazy enough to be mayor for eight years."

The venue was perfect for the town's oldest professional sports lineage to enter a brand-new era, finally officially acknowledging that every era of the Earthquakes—from 1974 straight through the "in-between 1980s" and now MLS—was all part of one family. With the team's new stadium taking shape a few miles up the road and across from Mineta San Jose International Airport, every trajectory from the team's different historical eras finally seemed to be converging.

And for the party, the Quakes went all out. After spending four months assembling a video montage of forty years' worth of Earthquakes history, the team projected the video on large screens gracing two buildings, the Fallon House and the SunWize tower across the street. In another example of everything coming full circle, the latter building is currently home to the law offices of Easy Perez, who the Quakes originally drafted out of San Jose State University in 1979.

As the night unfolded, thousands gathered en masse in the streets to watch Johnny Moore talk about the original 1974 squad and how the current team somehow managed to carry on the working-class, never-say-die spirit of those original squads. Current president Dave Kaval officially revealed the team's new logo, jersey and branding concepts, and San Jose civic leaders gave their obligatory speeches.

Former MLS players like Troy Dayak also took the podium to rally the crowd. In particular, Dayak told his own emotional saga of being the first MLS player ever traded in 1996, when he refused to play in New Jersey, essentially forcing a deal so he could play for San Jose instead. The crowd roared with enthusiasm.

The San Jose Earthquakes fortieth anniversary party in San Pedro Square, San Jose. *John Todd/ISI Photos; San Jose Earthquakes.*

After the team's new jersey and logo were revealed, crowds continued to meander in and out of the market area, where several glass cases presented paraphernalia and ephemera from the NASL days, through the WSL and the Blackhawks eras and straight up to modern times. Also inside the market area, across the floor from the glass case displays, members of the 1974 team—Moore, Mani Hernandez, Art Welch and Davie Kemp—answered questions on stage from Chris Dangerfield. So many people jammed the confines that it was difficult to even hear what was going on.

Then came the quintessential San Jose punk rock conclusion—or perhaps, concussion—to finish off the night. As was propagandized from the very beginning, Rancid guitarist Lars Frederiksen, a native of nearby Campbell who had grown up with the NASL Quakes, performed with his side band, the Old Firm Casuals. Now, as a forty-three-year-old fan of the current team and one who still attends matches whenever he's not touring, Frederiksen wrote the official San Jose Earthquakes theme song, as performed by the Old Firm Casuals. To close out the party, the band played a thirty-minute set, including officially debuting the new theme song, "Never Say Die." They even played it twice. With street-punk fervor and gritty harmony, the song celebrated the Earthquakes' working-class ethic and its never-give-up attitude while lampooning the more flashy identities of New York and Los Angeles in the lyrics.

Inspired by British Oi! music, the Old Firm Casuals seemed a logical fit for a working-class team's signature track. Since the very beginnings of that music, it has been inseparable from football. Also, since many of the MLS Earthquakes' marketing schemes during previous years had seemed hokey and bush-league, to say the least, this partnership was homegrown and dovetailed perfectly. Now the team had a world-renowned guitarist who had grown up with the team, grown up with soccer, writing a song for the team in a style of music historically connected with football. It was real punk rock, real football music and a strong antidote to the gaudy, ad brochure–looking schlock inflicted on the league via Nike.

On stage, Frederiksen talked about growing up with the NASL incarnation of the Earthquakes. "George Best came to my school when I was a kid," he said at the microphone. "And he smelled of liquor."

Frederiksen, who's been sober for twenty years, also devoted one song to his deceased brother, "Rocking Rob" Dapello, without whom Lars said he would never have discovered punk rock or soccer. But that was still not an end to the borderline-mystical degrees of convergence embroidering this entire thread. Gavin O'Brien, singer for San Jose's most famous punk band, The

Lars Frederiksen of Rancid (left), along with guest singer Gavin O'Brien of 1980s San Jose skate punk legends The Faction, performing at the San Jose Earthquakes fortieth anniversary party, January 30, 2014, San Pedro Square Market. *Napoleon Badillo.*

Faction, from back in the 1980s, who also grew up with the original NASL team, then jumped in with the band to guest-sing two Faction songs, all while decked out in a red Earthquakes jersey. The entire night was probably the most "San Jose" event I had seen in many years.

Easy Perez told me he was blown away by the huge party of thousands in the streets and how everything had now come full circle. Especially poignant was the irony of projecting video from the last forty years of San Jose soccer on the side of a building that just happens to house his office. "We made it," he declared, reflecting on decades' worth of San Jose soccer births, deaths and rebirths. "After we thought it was going to fizzle away, it came back with the teams Laurie [Calloway] had, the Blackhawks and Bridgwater's teams. So it wanted to start up again, but it really couldn't take off…the money just wasn't there. But then MLS came along and the team gets transferred to Houston, and you thought, 'Here we go again.' But luckily the name stayed here. Wolff came in and it started again, and now we have our own stadium. We made it. Soccer is here to stay."

Throughout 2014, the Quakes released video after video on the team's website, celebrating forty years of their heritage. Several characters among these pages spoke of their own personal histories with the team in every incarnation, every era. All of this ramped up the public's awareness of the official fortieth anniversary celebration that erupted over the May 10 weekend. Nearly forty years to the day of the original NASL San Jose Earthquakes' inaugural home game on May 11, 1974, the MLS Quakes played FC Dallas. That same night, Johnny Moore was inducted into the team's hall of fame, bringing yet another circle to its completion. (Full disclosure: I was among those on the induction committee.)

To celebrate Moore's induction, several original 1974 teammates, mostly the ones who still lived in the area, threw a party the night beforehand at SP2 Communal Restaurant in San Pedro Square. Paul Child flew out from the East Coast to attend. Krazy George also attended, chowing down on gourmet hors d'oeuvres with everyone else. Several younger Quakes alumni, including Joe Cannon and Dave Salzwedel, also showed up in support of Moore. After everyone had tipped a few back, the party moved around the corner to Britannia Arms, where two cakes inscribed in Johnny's name awaited.

As the Quakes' fortieth anniversary year unfolded through the summer of 2014, a profound convergence of synchronicities on multiple levels showcased the ways in which the entire four-decade saga had finally come full circle. The ancient Eastern mystics would have used all sorts of terminology to describe the circular processes of birth, death, rebirth, reincarnation or cause-and-effect relationships resulting in the particular sequence of events at the end of July and beginning of August. Far beyond conventional linear Western concepts of time, with a tinge of Laughing Buddha–style bliss, allow me to suggest it was quite deep.

On July 27, the Earthquakes played an exhibition match against Atletico Madrid at Candlestick Park in San Francisco as part of the 2014 Copa Euroamericana. It was the last sporting event ever played at the storied yet crumbling stadium, which was soon to be demolished. "The Stick," as it came to be known, housed the San Francisco Giants from 1958 to 1999 and the 49ers from 1971 to 2014. Just six days later, on August 2, the Quakes played the opening event at Levi's Stadium in Santa Clara, the brand-new home of the 49ers. That same weekend, in a supposedly unrelated occurrence, both former mayor Norman Mineta and pop star Dionne Warwick were back in San Jose as part of a conference devoted to citizen diplomacy. The day

Members of the 1974 San Jose Earthquakes celebrating their fortieth anniversary in 2014. *Top row, left to right*: Mark Demling, Johnny Moore, Paul Child, Davie Kemp. *Front row, crouching*: Krazy George. *Gary Singh.*

before the Quakes opened the Niners' new facility, Warwick played a concert at the Center for Performing Arts, including a rousing rendition of "Do You Know the Way to San Jose?" When contemplating the meaning of such a grand sequence of events unfolding during the Quakes' fortieth anniversary

The San Jose Earthquakes played the inaugural match at Levi's Stadium, the new home of the San Francisco 49ers. *John Todd/ISI Photos; San Jose Earthquakes.*

season, it is difficult to remain practical, pragmatic, realistic or logical. The ways in which these events brought everything full circle were just too mind-blowing for rational analysis.

Forty years earlier, the San Jose Earthquakes had begun by hiring Dick Berg away from his job as the 49ers promotions director. Gabbo Gavric had even been a place kicker for the 49ers during the 1969 season. Now the Quakes were playing the last game at Candlestick, officially closing the old 49ers stadium, and then opening the new 49ers stadium the following weekend. Norm Mineta had been mayor when the Quakes began. Warwick's tune was the backdrop at that time. Now both of them were back in town.

What's more, before the Quakes played the inaugural match at Levi's Stadium, Dick Berg himself kicked out the first ball, completing the circle of history unlike anything anyone could possibly have predicted. In other words, the guy who helped the 49ers move into Candlestick from Kezar, and who then helped start the original San Jose Earthquakes in 1974, was now opening the new 49ers stadium forty years later, along with the current San Jose Earthquakes. It didn't seem real. Berg was giddy just reflecting on everything. "Of all the stuff I have done in sports and on fields for whatever reason, I have never been the sole person in front of forty-eight thousand people," Berg said. "I couldn't have been prouder of my past, you might say. This was magnificent—wouldn't have changed a thing."

Somewhere between the Tao of Physics, Hindu mysticism, Ayahuasca scholarship and several Alan Watts YouTubes, there's a lost metaphor about all points converging at key moments in history. August 2, 2014, felt like one of those moments. Several trajectories from the club's past came spiraling back to the forefront, possibly as a cosmic way to close out one era while simultaneously cracking open the next one. All of this took place just as the Quakes were starting to prepare for their own brand-new facility—that is, just as they were gearing up for their first-ever permanent home, Avaya Stadium, across from Norman Mineta San Jose International Airport.

But there just had to be something else. As if everything previously mentioned wasn't already cyclical enough, as if history hadn't already repeated itself in multiple layers, one last remaining piece of space-time continuum-shattering madness needed to happen in order to bring the entire San Jose Earthquakes' forty-year experience to a grand conclusion.

On October 15, 2014, just as I was about to finish this book, the San Jose Earthquakes announced that Dominic Kinnear would return as head coach following the conclusion of the 2014 season. In the press conference announcing his return, Kinnear harkened back to the first times he ever attended Earthquakes games in the NASL era, as a kid: "Really, my first memory was the dirt hill behind the goal—just kind of watching the game from that dirt hill, sliding down, running back up and watching the game and sliding back down again. That takes it back quite a ways, when soccer really wasn't at the forefront of my mind and it was just about going to the game and watching."

Now, Kinnear would be coming back home after a successful nine-year run as Houston's only coach, the one who essentially built the entire club and turned the team into everything it currently is today. Rarely in MLS does any coach last that long at the helm. When one thinks back to the day when the Quakes originally moved to Houston, especially since Kinnear should have stayed in Texas only until the Quakes reemerged, his ultimate return—just in time for a new stadium to open and a new era to commence—seemed to wrap a bow around the whole forty-year package.

As the curtain on the first forty years drew to a close, the proverbial stage crew was setting the show for the next four decades. Just as one era was concluding, another one was about to begin. This is often how history works. When great stories come to an end, they tend to leave us with brand-new stories.

The Boys Are Back

Earlier in the spring of 2014, when the Quakes inducted Johnny Moore into the team's hall of fame, original Quakes players from the 1970s had taken a hardhat tour of Avaya Stadium that weekend, as its construction took shape. On that Saturday afternoon, Moore, Paul Child, Mark Demling, Jim Zylker, Davie Kemp, Lalo Perez and several others explored the multimillion-dollar facility. "We all had the same expression, and we all talked about it afterwards," Moore said. "It was like, 'We're part of this. You know, this is what we built.' Now, we may be a very small part of it, but when we started [this club], it was hard to imagine that forty years later, they'd be building the very first actual home that we own—that the club owns."

Moore couldn't imagine Glasgow Celtic building a club and then not building a stadium until forty years later. In the old country, it simply didn't work that way. But in San Jose, it apparently did.

"It was a great feeling," Moore said. "We stood in the middle of the field and looked around, and it was magnificent. If you look at the sightlines, there's not a bad seat in the house. The noise is going to be rocking. If you looked ahead five years, this could be Seattle, where you can't absolutely get a ticket, but it's only eighteen thousand and they're standing on top of each other. This would be the thing that finally cements the club."

That weekend, Demling first saw the stadium construction as he arrived at Mineta San Jose International Airport. One can easily see the stadium from inside the terminal. All one has to do is look westward across Coleman Avenue, and there it is. Seeing the team's future venue from the airport, Demling knew it was real this time. After having played through the NASL era, with teams folding and/or relocating every single year, and then suffering remotely through the Quakes' move to Houston and their protracted expansion tenure at Buck Shaw, his pessimism finally evaporated. "After seeing it, my biggest thing was, 'The franchise is not going to leave now,'" Demling recalled. "Honestly, that was my biggest fear. I flew in, I landed at the airport and I could see it. I can remember getting off the plane, and I just stood there at the window because I could see it. I just looked out the window and said, 'Oh, man, the steel is up. It's there, and it's not going anywhere.'"

Moore agreed: "Suddenly you went, 'They can't go back now. It's here.' Because regardless of what happens, the franchise has put a foothold in. And it's real. And the stadium is a huge reward for anybody that's ever played for the club at any point. It's the combination of everybody's efforts."

As the 1974 squad continued to reflect on it, I got the feeling that they had been harboring just as much anxiety as the fans, in regards to whether a new stadium would ever finally happen. And now that it was indeed happening, they were just relieved more than anything.

"It doesn't do me any good to say, 'Hey, I helped build this,' if nothing's there," Demling said. "So if they move the team again and nothing's there, what can I say that I did? Now I feel that what we did in the beginning has led to something. It's led to a permanent foundation. And they spent a lot of money on it."

As Kemp put it, "This is a long way from Spartan Stadium, where you got splinters in your butt while sitting on the bench, or in the training room and those crappy showers we had. We've come a long way." Child concurred, adding that Avaya Stadium dwarfed what the 1974 team could ever have imagined. That was forty years earlier, back when they used to nosh on steaks at Los Gatos Lodge before every game. "They [now] have a cook that cooks them special food," Child said. "They have a games room. They have the fitness center. They have their trainer's equipment. Outside the garage doors, there's fields. It's like a dreamland. I think a lot of us just looked at each other and thought, 'Boy, if we'd had even a third of what these blokes are getting in this training facility, just think how good we could have been.'"

DECADES IN THE MAKING

Late one sunny morning in the fall of 2014, Britannia Arms on Almaden Expressway seemed tranquil as the lunch crowd had yet to arrive. The sun beat down on the half-empty parking lot. On my way into the pub, I stood and looked across the lot at the monolithic cement overpass of Highway 85, stretching over the horizon toward the southeastern expanses of San Jose. A ubiquitous roar of highway traffic blanketed the scene. It was easy to recall the days when members of the San Francisco Bay Blackhawks tended bar at this pub twenty-three years ago, before that freeway existed.

After I made it inside, the proprietor and I stood at the bar as I drank tea with a decades-long regular customer, who sat on the other side of me. Originally from the same Belfast neighborhood as George Best, he and I began to trade stories from every era of the San Jose Earthquakes. Together, the three of us marveled at how far the lineage had come. As we contemplated the new stadium, located across from the airport named after the first Asian American mayor in the United States, who just happened to be mayor when the Quakes first started, we almost felt the goose bumps growing. Some people out there have probably been waiting decades for this to happen, we thought.

It was amazing, we also thought, that people are still talking about Krazy George in his helicopter, about that famous George Best goal, about Laurie Calloway's feud with Eric Wynalda and about Yallop and Kinnear's two championships, Landon Donovan's legacy and Chris Wondolowski's clinical poaching talents all in the same San Jose conversation. It's no different than people in the bars of St. Louis talking about Stan Musial, Ozzie Smith and Pujols all in the same conversation.

San Jose now has a forty-year tradition, a multilayered professional sports bloodline, a series of aftershocks and ripple effects from what Milan Mandaric and Dick Berg started along with the entire 1974 side. From that year until now, everyone who played for any of the teams in any year; everyone who schlepped equipment or collected loose soccer balls at practices; every kid who ever showed up and hung around; every front office staff member, ad rep or communications person; and anyone who was ever part of any incarnation for the last forty years—each one of them is an inseparable piece of the stadium that now sits across from the Mineta San Jose International Airport.

Will history repeat itself? Well, that's what the next forty years are for.

ABOUT THE AUTHOR

G ary Singh is an award-winning travel journalist with a music degree who publishes poetry, paints and exhibits photographs. As a journalist, he's published nearly one thousand works, including travel essays, art and music criticism, profiles, business journalism, lifestyle articles and more. Every week for ten years, he has written the "Silicon Alleys" column for *Metro*, San Jose's alternative weekly newspaper. As a kid in San Jose, he played soccer from ages seven to fourteen.

Visit us at
www.historypress.net

....

This title is also available as an e-book